Praise for

Vietnam 1971

Remembering The 101st *Then* And *Now*

"After reading the book I am now not ashamed of what I did. I am also proud to say I am a Viet Nam Vet. I did what my country asked me to do. Thank you for helping me to come to terms with this."
Steve Exline, Vietnam Veteran.

"Everyone should write a story like this. It is a part of Americana that's missing. This book may be the new gold standard for Vietnam books—from someone who has read them all. Every Vietnam Vet should have this book and it should be in the PX at Ft. Campbell, Kentucky." **Fred Monahan, Past National Commander, Legion of Valor, U.S. Marines, Vietnam Veteran.**

"The Vietnam War era was a very difficult period for those of us who lived through it. Some of us believed we best served the country by supporting the war, others by serving in the war, or still others by protesting the war through peaceful means. We need to move past all of that now and hopefully we have learned significant lessons to help us avoid repeating history. Many, many casualties resulted from the war and some soldiers and their families are still bearing the burden of a war's cost. Those who died or are still a Prisoner of War or Missing in Action must not be forgotten. Lives, careers, families, and dreams that were lost, destroyed, or disrupted cannot be fully assessed or valued. Jim's book captures the spirit of the times but doesn't assess blame. It is more a forward looking memoir necessary for the continued healing of a country and individuals. It's a non-gory book that is a very good read."
Russ Knapp, Vietnam War Protester.

"My brother Tommy was drafted in the Spring of 1968, despite his status as a young married and a full time student. He had no military nature, being the easy-going and low key type. I do not know why he chose to not resist the draft, as my older brother had done. He just gave in and went to Vietnam and died six months later.

I have, to some degree, never fully recovered from his death. I also have an Uncle on my Mom's side, whom I never met. He served in the Calgary Highlanders and fell in the D-Day Invasion of Normandy in June 1944. He is buried in France.

Two different wars, as vastly different as night and day. I dealt with my brother's death by heading full force into the peace movement in my youth (I was 15 when my brother was killed) and while the peace movement gave a vent for my emotions, it did nothing to make the pain go away. Humans still behave badly, all over the place.

Except for the sincere following of faith in God and seeking the reason for human existence, war is the huge shaping structure of all of human history. I would imagine there have been thousands of wars on every continent, both large and small.

At nearly age 64, I work now part time in a library. As a writer myself and an inveterate researcher and curious girl, I see many many books with stories of one conflagration after another, the staggering toll of humans arguing with one another on the field of battle. The civilian population is always in the middle and suffers a blow from all sides.

If I did not have faith in God and His Son Jesus Christ, I could not have continued through my life. Despite my wanderings, I know there is a purpose to life and I fervently pray I will see my dear brother again when I have left this world.

Many sincere thanks to Mr. Cheskawich for making the effort to write this important book and to share his personal experiences in serving in Vietnam. I believe only a fellow veteran can understand what someone went through in any war." ***Wendy E. Williams, On-Line Researcher, Writer/Author.***

"Dear Jim, I had tears in my eyes while working with you on your book. You have humanized the War for me. Thank you." *Vicki Weiland, Editor, Vietnam 1971; Editor, Rex: The Blizzard King.*

"I thank you for the respectful way that you treated my poem." *Mike Viehman, Author, "Visit to the Wall."*

"For someone like me who was fortunate enough to have a student deferment during the draftable portion of the Viet Nam War, this book is just what I have needed all these years! I never wanted to be involved with the war, except of course for some student demonstrations in the spring of 1970, so I have always felt a little guilty that I never served my country during that time. I got to graduate on a Saturday and start my full time 40-year government job the very next Monday. No disrupted life for me! This book allows me to understand so much more! The author took me there with him. This book is so real and fascinating. I loved every part of it! The author has a gift telling his story!

You know the feeling you get when watching certain movies where you just forget totally about your own life and then you are affected by it for many days thereafter. This book did that for me. Just a great read!"
Dave Sage, Meteorologist and Photographer.

"After reading your book on your Vietnam experience it brought back memories of the music, media and the culture of that era. It reminded me of the friends and relatives that served during the war and helped me to better understand the trials and difficulties of not just being there, but also of facing the harsh realities they confronted with coming home. On a personal note it made me think of my son Zach who spent 5 combat tours in Iraq and returned to a world here at home that was very difficult for him to adjust to. Zach would open up at times to me, but he really relied on his brothers and sisters that he served with to understand and counsel him. Jim has written an excellent book that I thoroughly enjoyed."
Randy Martinez, Educator, Football and Softball Coach; father of an Iraq Combat Warrior.

"As a combat Veteran who served two tours in a 'Search and Rescue' Unit in North Vietnam, rescuing or assisting in the rescue of what I recall as nine U.S. Navy pilots shot down while on bombing runs over North Vietnam, I appreciate and thank you, Jim, for your Service, and for sharing your experience in *Vietnam 1971*, your well-written book about *Remembering The 101ˢᵗ Then And Now.*" **Jim Weiland, USN 1965-1967.**

"Growing up the Vietnam Conflict was all around me—yet it never 'touched' me. My much older brother-in-law survived his tour and was home by the time I was 10. I recall images on the nightly news of young American boys fighting in an unrecognizable tangle of jungles an elusive enemy in defense of an even more elusive objective. American Boys—and they were just boys, some too young to vote—had their once potentially noble destinies undermined and dreams crushed because they couldn't or wouldn't dodge the draft. They were all sacrificial lambs sent to slaughter or be slaughtered. I remember it as being extremely unpopular. I remember the protests. I remember the universal chants for peace. I remember my Father, a WWII veteran, being outraged over the protests. He possessed an unflinching loyalty to his beloved country. To him, the protesters and draft dodgers were traitors. All Americans knew, hated and wanted to avenge the villains of WWII. But who were the Viet Cong? What did they do to or how were they threatening us? It was all such a mystery. I remember being relieved when the conflict—this costly and undeclared war—was resolved before any of my high school friends were drafted. But, as horrific and senseless as this conflict was, I was too young, too lucky and too protected to have it ruin my childhood and early adulthood. I got to fulfill my dreams and live happily ever after.

Vietnam 1971 is a captivating and honestly written memoir of a soldier—a son of a World War II veteran and a boy much too young, too naïve and too American to question his family's and country's expectations. It is the author's insightful, poignant and noble treatise about how, through grit, ingenuity, good common sense and humor, he managed to survive a nightmarish experience and learn enough about human nature, protocol and politics to survive the aftermath. It is a heroic effort.

I never got the chance to learn about this conflict in high school — thank you, Jim, for your perspective and for the history lesson. Your exquisitely personal account 'touched' me. Your story is a brilliant testament to what was both good and bad about the 1960s and early 1970s." ***Annie Reid, Artist and Professional Legal Work.***

"I have started reading your manuscript and enjoyed it. My unit in Vietnam, the 192nd Assault Helicopter Company, was part of the First Aviation Brigade but we supported the 3rd BN, 506th, 101st. Most of my flying time in Vietnam was working for the 3/506th at Phan Thiet." *Jim Schueckler, Founder and President, www.VirtualWall.org, Ltd. The Virtual Wall™*

"After successfully surviving multiple deployments to various theatres of operations overseas and struggling each time to transition once getting back home, one clear message will forever resonate from my experiences. It is not about what I have done or seen, it is about our brothers in arms who didn't get the opportunity to come home. By not only sharing our stories and putting our experiences into words, we are honoring the fallen and are giving them the opportunity to live once again. No one shared those precious moments with them like we did and to not keep their story alive is to fail in honoring their existence and sacrifice. This book as well as our memories are a testament to preserving those who made the ultimate sacrifice, 'lest we forget.' Thank you once again, Mr. Cheskawich." *Anonymous, as requested.*

"I was very moved by Jim Cheskawich's memoir about Vietnam. It gave a new perspective on the Vietnam War and it proved that 'good' can come out of any experience, even war. I had always 'kept my distance' from the subject of Vietnam but I found myself riveted to Jim's observations and I enjoyed all his personal anecdotes from his unusual vantage point of being a soldier in an 'office.'

I am glad that Jim Cheskawich has told his story and if it was therapeutic for him to write, it will be therapeutic for others to read. I hope other Vietnam Vets and their families and friends will read this book. I recommend it." **Minette Siegel, Photographer and Media Consultant. Former Partner in The Studio of David Inocencio/Minette Siegel (multimedia filmmakers). Image Director for *Vietnam 1971* and *Rex, The Blizzard King.***

"My time in Viet Nam changed the way I would look at life forever. We were young flight attendants assigned to work on military charter (MAC) flights taking troops home from the war zone, or returning them from leave between Saigon and Travis Air Force Base in Northern California. Some were lucky to be going home for good. Often, the hot rainy and windy weather turned our sky rides into a formidable roller-coaster with beverages plastering themselves onto the ceiling. Listening to the GI's laugh and enjoy the hard ride always gave me a sense of pride that they were certainly brave souls. Sometimes a look on a face will tell you all you need to know—that war is hell and the best you can do is talk about life back home to help them forget. 'Yes, the A's won the pennant,' or 'Yes, you saw the Miami Dolphins win the Super Bowl.'

Once we were ordered off the plane in haste as Intelligence had it that a North Vietnamese offensive was on the way to Saigon. Ushered onto a team of small helicopters (Hueys) we could see the enemy troops in the jungle below looking up and shooting at us. Some of the bullets were hitting the Huey and causing a loss of fuel, but, thankfully, we made it to the intended airfield on fumes. All I could think of was how awful it would be to crash in the jungle and face the enemy, if we did survive. What about the brave soldiers who face it every day? Seeing war up-close and personal, my heart changed forever, knowing what is at stake to save civilian lives like mine. Someone must go into that dense jungle facing death or torture! Do any of us deserve their bravery, ever?

I saw anti-war demonstrations at home, and yes we all wanted it to end, but not at the expense of treating the military personnel so badly as people trying to make them feel they were 'outcasts' from society just for being in Viet Nam. It was their turf, not ours. That jungle made people crazy and the war drug out too long, but, eventually, we began taking civilians out of Saigon as well. The fear on their faces was telling, many pleading with us to take more of them on board, and trying to pay us to hide them in the closets and restrooms. We refused to be paid. No more can I say. Babies must be held on laps during take-off and landing. With seven flight attendants, you have seven laps, but I never said that. What Manifest? In the early Spring of 1975, I was on one of the last Trans America Airlines flights out of Saigon, light on luggage and heavy on precious cargo, with pilots with big hearts. Knowing what happened to those we left behind, I will always wish we had won. I believe the Viet Nam Memorial had to happen. It should have been sooner. Soldiers don't start wars; they just go to finish them. You never forget the faces of war or the brave hearts that try so hard to do their job. The least I could do is be kind." ***Judith Gail Lund, Senior Flight Attendant, Trans America Airlines, TIA/TAA, Oakland and New York, 1969 to 1978.***

"I was a college student at U.C. Berkeley and many of us there thought we 'could change the world.' I personally was tired of my friends coming home in 'body bags' when there seemed to be no reason for it. One night in 1967, my boyfriend and I decided to join a March to close down the Oakland (California) Army Induction Center. Knowing we would be up all night, we took 'speed' to stay awake. We were some of the first to arrive and ended up at the head of the crowd, feeling alive and powerful. Directly across the intersection, the police began to amass, clothed in their riot gear, billy clubs and all.

We waited all night and into the early morning, blocking the building. Then with no warning, the police began to move toward us very fast, forming a 'V-shape' into the crowd, swinging their clubs. Like Moses parting the Sea, we were forced up against the building, being struck many times, running the gauntlet. After this, many kept at it. I didn't. Didn't feel so powerful after all!

This memoir about the war in Vietnam should be read by Veterans and their families and friends, as the War affected all of us, and a lot of healing has not begun. " ***Kitty Hastings, Photographer.***

"Dear Jim, it seems like we just 'Facebooked' the other day. I must go back to see what I said about Vietnam and how I felt about the nightmare our troops endured.

My most-clear memory (and it was like it was yesterday!) was the low-key manner in which our soldiers were sent to Vietnam. The protesters seemed to capture all of the headlines. It was disgraceful and I felt so sad for this 'understated War,' lack of preparation, lack of weaponry and supplies . . . I often felt they were fighting with one hand tied behind their back!

Actually, this whole period of the Vietnam War seemingly exuded a LACK OF SUPPORT for our men and women in harm's way. What a debacle. It was even worse upon their return. The stories told and revolved around 'the questionable' tactics of our guys: how the children were killed, villages burned and blown-up . . . no mention of what our troops had to endure. Yes, I understand security . . . it was, HOWEVER, a very lopsided and poorly planned, entry and exit. We did not receive our returning soldiers with support (physically or emotionally), honor, or distinction.

My heart is heavy when I reflect. The longer I continue reflecting on this period, the more I feel myself getting agitated. And, I KNOW Vietnam Vets—some have been the parents of my students, some I see on the street and it is heartbreaking, Jim!!! Some were friends from high school who served in Vietnam, and, of course, Jim, some did not return.

BLESS your heart Jim Cheskawich, and *Rex, The Blizzard King* (the Book, and the Dog, whom you credit) for inspiring this project. THANK YOU for YOUR Service. I appear to lack the 'just right' words to honor you and your splendid creativity." ***Lindy Ward, Educator and Samoyed Owner.***

"Vietnam: 1971 is an interesting story about one person's tour of duty in a country thousands of miles from his personal comfort zone where he had lived most of his life. As a young draftee, fresh out of college, the author is challenged to instantly shift gears and adapt to a new, military based culture, totally different from one that he has ever experienced. Prior to the Vietnam conflict, most wars could be rationalized away in that they were fought over the age-old principle of good vs. evil. With Vietnam, for some, that was never quite clear and toward the end, there was little actual support for continuing the effort, with seemingly little chance of a clear-cut victory.

Jim Cheskawich focuses on one person's journey through his military obligation and what it was like to spend a year "in-country" at a place that absolutely no one could call home. He brings the reader along with him on his journey and helps open up a world to us that most have never experienced. The author goes on to describe how he was able to successfully return to civilian life after military service, to enroll in graduate school and to achieve positions of responsibility in the Federal sector. He also mentions his ability to "shift gears" and enter a whole new world of competitive dog breeding and showing. At the end, I found it to be a good read." ***David and Marion Gustafson.***

**Author on vacation in Florida in 2016, with a
"screaming eagle" that has *landed*!**

Vietnam 1971

Remembering The "101ˢᵗ" *Then* And *Now*

By Jim Cheskawich

Phu Bai, South Vietnam, 1971.
Shown are the storage facilities and the large helicopter pad
for the 101st Airborne Division.
Multiple helicopters can be seen on and around
the launch pad area.

"Camp Campbell," Phu Bai, South Vietnam, 1971.

"Most would agree that Vietnam was a highly unpopular war and that strong disagreements exist even today—50 years later—on both personal and U.S. policy levels. At the urging of fellow Vietnam Vets, my editor, and the teachers and school students I now work with, it is time to put down in writing what the War meant to me and how it changed my life.

I know where I came from, won't forget my roots, and cannot speak for anyone but myself." —**Jim Cheskawich**

COPYRIGHT

Vietnam 1971: Remembering The "101st" *Then* And *Now*

Developmental Editing and Design: Vicki Weiland
Text Editing and Proofreading: Jim Cheskawich
Image Director: Minette Siegel
Illustrated Maps: Brad Johnson
Manager, Book Layout and Interior Design: Desta Garrett Book Design
Book Formatting and Transfer Design: Kristie Kempker, Visually Speaking

Front Cover Photo: "Hueys on a Combat Air Assault,"
by *Randy Parmley* (Charlie Company, C/2/506th, c1970–71)
www.company-c--2nd-bn-506th-inf.com

Front Cover Photo: "Vietnam Memorial Wall" by *Tamara Somerville,* 2013
Vietnam Wall Memorial Sculptures by *Glenna Goodacre* (Nurses with Injured Soldier)
and *Frederick Hart* (Three Soldiers)
Photographs by *Carl Gernazio.*

With deepest appreciation to *Judy Collins,* her team of Erin Bockman and Katherine DePaul at
rockymountainproductionsinc.com and Troy Schreck on behalf of Alfred Publishing Company
for permission to use the lyrics of *Sons of* by Brel, Jouannest, Blau, Shuman, Editions Pouchenel,
S.P.R.L. and Unichappell Music, Inc.

Also thanks and appreciation to Lorraine Goonan, The Image Works, NY, for making available
ETPM0272986 and ENVO0756655. Also, Catharine Giordano from "Stars and Stripes."

Thanks also to Elise Gochberg and Marlous Fehr of Friesens.

And to *Bob Dylan*, the greatest songwriter and singer who spoke for our generation, and his team of
Jeff Rosen and Callie Gladman, for permission to use the lyrics to *All Along the Watchtower.*
Also to the late *Muhammad Ali* and his staff for photo of Muhammad Ali - Sonny Liston.
And to *Baron Wolman* for his portraits of Janis Joplin, Jimi Hendrix, and Bob Dylan.

A portion of the proceeds of this book will go to *Penn State University's Veterans Special Needs
Endowment Scholarship.*

Website to contact author: www.101stvietnam.com

Rex the BLIZZARD King Stories, LLC
ISBN 978-0-9883640-3-5
Printed in Canada by Friesens.

VIETNAM 1971

REMEMBERING THE "101ST" *THEN*

AND *NOW*

by Jim Cheskawich

REX THE BLIZZARD KING STORIES, LLC
November 2016
Printed in Canada by Friesens

"Sons of"

*"Sons of your sons, **sons passing by,***
Children were lost in lullaby.
Sons of true love, sons of regret,
All of your sons you can never forget.
Some built the roads, some wrote the poems,
Some went to war, some never came home.
*Sons of your sons, **sons passing by,***
Children were lost in lullaby."

Written by Gerard Jouannest, Jacques Roman Brel, Eric Blau and Mort Shuman,
©1968, (Renewed)
Editions Pouchenel, S.P.R.L. and Unichappell Music, Inc.
The song was performed by Judy Collins in 1970, in her classic album,
Colors of the Day, THE BEST OF *Judy Collins.*

**"In honor of all who served,
and those who never came home."**

Judy Collins in Concert.
With thanks and appreciation to
Lorraine Goonan, The Image Works, Inc., NYC.

DEDICATION

TO:

Larry Sindelar, *died March 5, 2011*

Dennis Lorenzini, *died February 23, 1969*

B. J. Moses, *died January 29, 2013*

Ron Dallam, *died September 4, 1988*

**And to all who served our country
in Vietnam and in the military.**

Vietnam Campaign Medal.

AUTHOR'S NOTE: These "love beads," made of Carnelian agate, were mined in Brazil in the 1850s. I bought them at a "Head Shop" in Escondido, California in 2007. When I wear them today, I am always *thinking of a different time*... sometimes *then*, in the 1970s and earlier, when all of us were so young... and sometimes *now*... some 50 years later.

WHY I WROTE THIS BOOK:

M y family and I were vacationing in the Berkshires at a timeshare in Hancock, Massachusetts during the late summer of 2013. I had just about given up writing about Vietnam as *I couldn't type a single word all week* on my laptop about it. I kept looking for excuses and diversions. During the last day for sightseeing, I drove up by myself to the Beacon which is at the highest point in the state of Massachusetts.

I was struck by the eagle carved into the granite monument and the words on the memorial: "… to honor Massachusetts men and women who had died during the World War…to honor the memory of fallen heroes…and (the Beacon) stands as a *timeless memorial to casualties of all wars."* I thought of my two friends in Vietnam from Massachusetts (I wondered if they made it home) and I made a commitment to *start that book* at the Albany airport *the very next day.*

Now that I have finished the book, I can understand more clearly the reason for memorials and monuments is so that *we never forget the sacrifices made to ensure our freedom.* There is good reason many feel that mandatory service to our country in some manner for one or two years is the price we pay for our freedom, and I agree. Otherwise, we tend to forget the costs and become complacent.

I hope that fellow Vietnam Vets and their families will find reading this book healing, and that other readers unfamiliar with war may gain perspective and understanding of what war is like from my journey of self-discovery ... which follows.

-- Jim

Scenes In or Near Phu Bai, 1971.

TABLE OF CONTENTS

***All Along the Watchtower* by Bob Dylan, 1968**

Map of North and South Vietnam, circa 1971, by Brad Johnson

Camp Evans by Randy Parmley

"THE KID IS COMING HOME" (Anonymous, circa 1968)
(AUTHOR'S NOTE: This is the "Sanitized Version" by me. Original Source is Unknown,
circa 1968–1970. Slightly different and even "politically correct" versions
appear on the Internet, but this is the version we had at Phu Bai.)

**"GS" (General Schedule) Levels and Military Rank Equivalencies
(Geneva Convention Categories)**

**Crowds at The Vietnam Memorial Wall, Washington, DC.
Photograph by Carl Gernazio**

**IN MEMORIAM: Sculpture by Glenna Goodacre
near The Vietnam Memorial Wall, Washington, DC. Photograph by Carl Gernazio**

Vietnam War Deaths by: Race, Service Branch, Service Component, and Age
From "Traveling Vietnam Memorial Wall."
Photographs by Celinda Cheskawich

"Gone, but not forgotten." Photograph by author

Map of Ho Chi Minh Trail, circa 1971, by Brad Johnson

"Albany Airport, NY." Photograph by Dave Sage

**"Traveling Vietnam Memorial Wall"
"...Brothers, you will go to THE Wall soon..."
Excerpt from Poem by Michael S. Viehman**

INTRODUCTION

SOARING WITH EAGLES IN THE GREAT BEYOND

J ust a week before commencing with the initial handwritten outline for my Vietnam memoir, I observed two bald, screaming eagles in determined flight over the top of my small orchard in Woodland, Washington. I had never seen bald eagles fly before, but I had seen plenty of hawks, falcons, owls, and crows in flight.

I raced upstairs and pulled out my binoculars which I had bought while in Vietnam in 1971, and watched the two eagles circle the large gray house to the left of me on the hill. It appeared to me that they knew I was watching them, and they were then quickly joined in succession by three more eagles that appeared from beyond the horizon. The five eagles were caught up in a thermal draft and performed their patterned dance—which I thought was meant just for me—in the gray and white clouds.

Later that afternoon, I asked Kay Ketchum (my friend and a Native American healer) what she thought of all this. (Kay also had helped me by locating some rare pictures of "Rex" for my first book). Kay reminded me that *the eagles soar the highest*, and in Native American belief the eagles take the prayers of the mortals on earth to the Creator. She concluded that I had to make my own interpretation of the five bald eagles dancing. Whatever it meant to me was most important and all that really mattered.

Over the next few days, I thought about the five dancing eagles I had witnessed, looked a few times at my Vietnam patch from the "Screaming Eagles of the 101st Airborne Division," and kept thinking—*I have a story to tell and I better get it down while I have the opportunity!*

Each of these pictures evoke long-held emotions of the Vietnam War period, which I survived but relive whenever I come into contact with impactful images such as these.

I want to thank Annie Reid of Suffield, Connecticut, for her Original Art, "Peace, Love, and Non-Violence."

My heartfelt appreciation and gratitude goes to the "Veterans of Foreign Wars," Robert Widener, Art director, *VFW Magazine* for the photograph, "Soldiers with the 173rd Airborne Brigade, serving in Vietnam as the first U.S. Army Ground Combat Unit."

And, for the enduring, eternally-moving photograph of caskets of U.S. Servicemen killed in an explosion in Vietnam, being unloaded at Travis Air Force Base in California on May 28, 1965, I am grateful to "Creative Commons" 4.0 CC License Suite, Public Domain Photograph, originally by Harry Groom, for *Newsweek Magazine*.

The "Daisy" photograph is by me, with the daisy taken from an arrangement purchased from the *Safeway* market near my home in Woodland, WA.

All of these flood me with memories set forth in my "journey"… which I am now about to share with you … my readers of all generations.

CHAPTER 1

Reflections:

Remembering Vietnam

———————————————

It has been nearly *forty-four years* since I finished my eleven-and-a-half-month tour with the 101st Airborne Division in Phu Bai, South Vietnam.

It has taken this extraordinarily long while to absorb and process the War to the point where I can now finally talk about what I experienced and how the War affected me. I could have published a diary or series of short stories soon after returning from Vietnam in 1972, but I hadn't experienced the full effect of the War on me yet and—at that time and up until recently—I wanted to get as far away from Vietnam as possible in my mind.

What has surprised me in writing this book is that I remember having other periods in my life that spanned several years or decades, such as some of my civilian jobs in later life—but I do not recall many details as I do from the War! After having been submerged for over *four decades*, I remember even the *smallest details* from my time with the 101st!

Those days of quick helicopter rides, frequent bunker line duty with my M-16 and flak jacket, regular diving for cover under anything that was not moving, "lookout towers" (Watchtowers), rusted concertina wire, *Stars and Stripes* newspaper, and off-color, brownish "vanilla" ice cream are still very easily recalled. Today, I still cannot figure out why that vanilla ice cream could not be *white*, even though it was a war…and even though I recognize that, surely, the little things in life become over-important sometimes, when adrift from all things familiar, and once comforting and taken for granted.

I have decided to *write* about it.

It is my hope that this book will serve as a catalyst to further healing and talking about Vietnam in the U.S. and that it will strongly appeal to those who lived during the '60s or '70s, or those who want to "view" up-close the life of a soldier in the Vietnam War zone

without getting tripped up by battle descriptions or killings.

This book is *one* soldier's report on what happened.

Most Veterans (Vets) have *not written* about their Vietnam experiences, will *not talk* about it, either, and we are left with Hollywood to give us the "real" inside story. Some of my Veteran friends told me recently that they were in the "Special Forces" and thus they still cannot talk about their assignments—even if they wanted to. Oliver Stone, as well as others who did serve in Vietnam, have brought their military experiences to the screen. However, most of us who served in Vietnam are not inclined to talk about the War to non-Vets, *ever*. Maybe there is some talk at military unit reunions, where, as one Vet told me, "Stories are exchanged and maybe a few embellishments are added on each year."

But I don't attend any reunions of my Unit, never did, and I gave up trying to contact anyone from my Personnel Branch of the 101st Administrative Company years ago, as the ones I did hear about had died, and usually from cancer.

To immediate family and friends, most of us just did not talk about the Vietnam War. I was no different. It wasn't as savage as the movie and book, *The Lord of the Flies,* but Vietnam does illustrate that when you have to "form, storm, norm (maintain established patterns of behavior), and perform" without full society serving as a buffer, feedback mechanism, or testing grounds, there are often dire results.

While married, I did not even talk to my *wife* about the War, except when I had dreams of being fired at with a gun or rifle, and my shouting woke her up!

But Vietnam has certainly been on my *mind, continually*, since I came back to the United States in early January of 1972 through Ft. Lewis, Washington.

In writing this book, one thing I knew for sure is that I didn't want it to be another saga of a depressing experience. That it certainly *was*.

I hope that this book will provide a unique perspective for readers. I do not want to repeat where others have gone. We have had enough of that now, out in the movies, books, on Internet sites, etc.

I do not believe that it is possible to spend a year in Vietnam without being changed very significantly in some way, either for good or bad. I believe that there has to be something good coming out of Vietnam, and it has taken me this long to be ready to examine my time there and find it.

Brotherhood and the healing of a country after the War ended are for sure positive aspects, but there are also the *individual stories of accomplishment*—and, for those fortunate enough to have lived through it, "moving on" from the War into productive lives stateside.

All of this needs to be told.

The War has been analyzed and reanalyzed so much that my purpose in writing is not to revisit all of the arguments and counter-arguments for being at war. I do not want to cover the major battles, skirmishes, and evolving war strategy. The generals and military experts, and especially those who served in the White House and Pentagon at the time, have that job.

A few years ago as a substitute teacher in La Center High School classes in southwest Washington State, the teachers and students started to "draw me out" and wanted to hear some real-life "oral history" about my first-hand experience stories and recollections about Vietnam. The first question most of the guys wanted an answer to was if I had *killed* anyone. After I quickly responded, "No," *then* they asked me if we had a drug problem over there, and, specifically, *if I "did" drugs*.

The class became *very quiet* when I talked about Vietnam, but I had to be *coaxed* into talking about the War, and it usually took me about 10–15 minutes before I got into any controversial or detailed descriptions of events. By the time I was warmed up, class was usually over, and I had to go through the same warm up for subsequent classes that day, as I couldn't just *dive into* the subject of my Vietnam service easily.

I think that the kids of today, especially, need to know what went on over there, and that gave me a reason to write my story. Some of my recollections may be construed as too honest, but I am willing to take that risk. And I know that I cannot blame every mistake I have made on the War, either.

"Memorial in the Field," Courtesy, Randy Parmley,
www.company-c--2nd-bn-506th-inf.com

VIETNAM WAR STATISTICS

In retrospect, and after review of the literature analyzing and summarizing the War events, Vietnam was quite simply in my view, a slaughterhouse. But until I finally saw the statistics, I was not fully aware of the high casualty rate and the strong arguments with supporting numbers that were used to show how the War was fought.

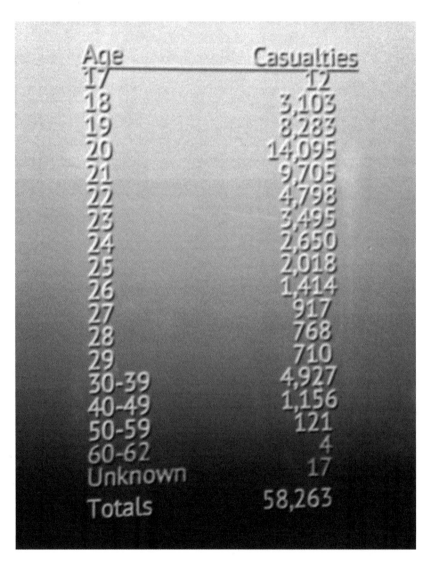

Age	Casualties
17	12
18	3,103
19	8,283
20	14,095
21	9,705
22	4,798
23	3,495
24	2,650
25	2,018
26	1,414
27	917
28	768
29	710
30-39	4,927
40-49	1,156
50-59	121
60-62	4
Unknown	17
Totals	58,263

**Photograph by Celinda Cheskawich,
Spring 2014, from "Traveling Vietnam Memorial Wall"
(built by John Devitt, Norris Shears, Gerry Hauer,
and other Vietnam Veterans volunteers).**

**AUTHOR'S NOTE: Of the 58,263 soldiers killed in the Vietnam War,
*35,198 (60.4%) were 21-years-old or younger.***

OVERALL:
The "Summary Raw Statistics" for
Those Serving in Vietnam

1. Vietnam Vets are 9.7% of their generation.

2. Deaths: 58,263.

3. Wounded: 303,704 (153,329 hospitalized and 150,375 injured requiring no hospital care).

4. Severely Disabled: 75,000.

5. 100% Disabled: 23,214.

6. Lost a Limb: 5,283.

7. Sustained Multiple Amputations: 1,081.

8. Missing in Action: 2,338.

9. Prisoners of War: 766 (114 died in captivity).

SOURCES: www.mddkw3.wix.com/Vietnam-Veterans, Mel Wallace, historian; statistics confirmed by *Vietnam for Dummies* and by U.S. Government Veterans Administration Statistics website.

While continuing my research for this book, I uncovered even more *startling* statistics. *Current statistics say* that of the 2.7 million who served, less than 850,000 (one-third) are alive today. Earlier statistics showed that *Vietnam Veterans, on average, were dying 10–12 years earlier (64–66 years old) than other males in the U.S. whose life-expectancy currently stands at age 76.*

Thus at age 68, I have outlived my Vietnam War Veterans' life-expectancy, and I am grateful for being a survivor!

I am writing this book for all Veterans who served, and especially for those who did not come home, or came home less than whole. (NOTE: A portion of the proceeds of the book will go to my *alma mater*, Penn State University, to the "Veterans Special Needs Endowment Scholarship.")

Remembering experiences, researching, and writing this book about the Vietnam War has been "life-changing" for me. It is **my hope** and **my Mission** that readers of this book will *feel* a deep connection, a deep release, and deep peace about it all ... *at last*.

**Fort Dix, Basic Training,
August–October 1970, age 22.**

This is what the book is all about—life before, during, and after the Vietnam War ... and continuing today. There are other Vietnam support staff servicemen and women who have written their own books, papers, or maintain their own websites and Facebook pages. Each of us has his or her story, along with personal lessons learned and choices taken.

If a Veteran takes the time to record his or her personal story, historians should appreciate the honesty!

Once all of us who served are *gone*, history will only be left with the "Raw Statistics and Summaries" of troop movements, which can be found currently in the textbooks and Internet sites used in classrooms. The *details* will be lost as to what it was like *day-to-day* performing the job you were assigned to do, or trained for, and then *waiting* to find out your destiny.

Classroom students need to know more about the horrors of war, the fear, and the costs of war on an individual and on society. Maybe then the future generations can keep us out of war better than my generation.

**Young troops in Da Nang
being entertained by equally young Vietnamese singers and musicians.**

PART ONE

How It Started For Me

"The Polish Falcon"

CHAPTER 2

I Never Expected to Get *Drafted* ...

So that we can follow how a "draftee" entered the War—and changed—it is important to view an individual's background for personality and personal attributes that might affect survival.

I am a third generation Lithuanian-Polish-American, with my Mom's side from near Krakow, Poland and my Grandfather (Vincent) coming over from Lithuania in 1904 on the *Hamburg* on a dead man's passport. The Russian Revolution was at hand and my Grandfather from Berzniki-Sejny wanted a better life for his family. He would be called today an "illegal alien." Both sets of grandparents came through Ellis Island in New York.

Because the name "*Czeszkiewicz*" was so hard to deal with in the new world and the Cyrillic alphabet version was even more cumbersome, the name was "Americanized" so we could fit in better in this new country and appease the masses in the great "Melting Pot." Sometimes, I want the original spelling of my name back and that would be in the Cyrillic alphabet.

> "84, Markiszki, (Lithuania),
> Birth Certificate of my Grandfather,
> Vincent CZESZKIEWICZ."

Growing up, I heard both Polish and Lithuanian spoken in my house. It is no wonder the experts said I was a slow reader in the first grade and my teacher placed me for two weeks in the "slow readers" group. I wasn't going to stay there any longer than I had to, and that was the minimum period. I learned to effectively "speed-read" later in life and became very competent at spelling, no doubt to overcompensate for an earlier difficulty.

My first grade report card also had checkmarks showing I did not always "work well with others." I think I started showing too much independence very early on and a probable disregard for school rules. I was paddled a few times: once for giving a kid a bloody nose and another time for tripping a different kid, thereby sending him sliding into the back wall. (Now I would probably be suspended from school—first graders do not do this stuff!) For the record, the kid in first grade did take my quarter in the restroom and I was not pleased. He was the class bully but he did not get away with too much with me.

Growing up in the country in Pangburn Hollow (it is not on the map, so don't even try to find it) which was between Elizabeth and Monongahela, Pennsylvania, I remember occasionally accompanying my Dad, Joseph (Joe), on small-game hunting trips up to the point in January of

Me, at about 9-months old, with my Godmother and aunt, Leona.

1958, when he passed away from his third heart attack at age 38. I was only age 9, and left with my Mom Eleanor (who died in 1986 from breast cancer), two younger brothers Bernie and Larry, and a younger sister Colleen. I used to babysit them all while my Mom went to Mass each Sunday.

My Dad served in World War II in the Pacific Theatre as a Sergeant and I have many uncles and cousins on both sides of the family who served in World War I and II, Korea, and Vietnam. We were probably lower middle class until my Dad died in 1958, and then, after he left, my Mom had to bring up the four of us on her own.

She had no job at the time and I remember years later asking her:

"Were we ever *lower class* at one point?

Of course, she said "*No,*"...but she *knew*....

We did, too.

My Dad in the Philippines, busy writing.

But she was determined that *we were going to succeed,* no matter the obstacles. We went through the Food Stamps: with surplus beans, cheese, peas, bacon, and milk, and sugar on mustard on white bread for some sandwiches. We were grateful for Lion's Club food donations, and for the Social Security payments which later made sure I had funding through college. We never lost the house and, as the oldest, I was entitled to try out all of the donated clothes *first!*

Adversity early on builds character, or you crumble. I didn't participate on a sports team in high school but I had a bicycle paper route and I worked as a bank teller at Western Pennsylvania National Bank my senior year of high school. In pick-up games I did enjoy tackling in football, rebounding in basketball, and playing baseball or softball.

I did not plan on going to college but my Mom said, "You ARE going!"

I wanted to work in the steel mill or coal mine like my Father, Grandfather, cousins, and uncles.

So M*om* applied to three community colleges *for* me!

The Penn State "Nittany Lion."

I chose Penn State's two-year community college at Fayette Campus, which was 30-miles away. While filling out the paperwork in Uniontown, I came across a space labeled "Graduate." I remarked to the Penn State contact that I wanted to graduate, of course! He laughed at me and said that it was a reference to graduate school and I was only in the two-year program. To be admitted to most graduate schools, he explained, you need four years of college first, and I was only in the two- year program.

Even so, he added, "You probably are not going to do well in the two-year program because your high school grade point average (GPA) is not what they would like to see, and you have no outside activities."

I did have a good score on the Scholastic Aptitude Test (SAT), but he said, "You will need to obtain a 3.50 GPA in your first term in the two-year program and then Penn State will let you convert to the four-year program." He paused and then continued, "However, I do not think you are going to make that."

I asked him, "Just give me a chance."

I do not remember if I told him that I never did homework in high school and did not study much for tests, even during study hall. (I had to work very hard later, though, to make up for my poor study habits while in high school; I hope no one does it the way I did back then, as that was the hard way.)

I had a 3.67 GPA my first term and I transferred over to the four-year college program. I had to start all over with new classes that were required for the B.S. in Management. I did not make any further mention to anyone at Penn State about "Graduate" for graduate school, but I never forgot it. First things first, and I had to get the four-year undergraduate degree.

At the main campus of Penn State from 1968–1970, I participated in intramural basketball and spent more time shooting baskets or playing pick-up basketball games at Recreation (Rec) Hall than I should have, instead of studying. Gene Wettstone (gymnastics coach) and Joe Paterno (football coach) noticed me at the Rec Hall so much that they probably thought I played for some other sports team with Penn State. I almost tried out for football at Penn State, but I let myself get talked out of it. It would have been something to say that I tried out but got cut the first day. It never happened, though.

Coach Gene Wettstone lived to be 100 and passed away in July of 2013.
He took Penn State to nine NCAA Gymnastics Championships,
and was known as "Mr. Gymnastics of the 1950s."
He was fond of quoting Thomas Jefferson:
"A strong body makes the mind strong,"
and that has stuck with me all of my life.

In basketball, I liked to rebound and considered it a good challenge to usually play at center. Somebody had to rebound and I did not mind bending my glasses out of shape or risk breaking them to *fight* for a rebound. (When I pick-up the "Sports Section" today and look at the statistics from a basketball game, I always look at the rebounds first before I look at who did the scoring.) I thought I was pretty good at basketball.

But I didn't see myself as a fighter who was supposed to go to Vietnam to shoot to kill the enemy!

"**...The team combat assaulted onto the roof of the embassy, searched every room and cubicle, and established a perimeter in the courtyard...**"

been captured by the enemy, who held it for 21 days. The 2nd Brigade troopers also participated in the battle to reclaim it, and one man, Sgt. Joe R. Hooper of the "Delta Raiders", 2nd Bn., 501st Abn. Inf., was awarded the Medal of Honor for his action (see pp. 22-23).

Meanwhile, it was decided to move the division to I Corps. Division headquarters and support battalions were airlifted north in late February and March, and the division fell under the guns of the 2nd Bn., 321st Arty., in one day.

Midway through the operation the 1st Brigade and the 1st Bn., 502nd Abn. Inf., were called to assist the 1st Cav in the first American strike into the A Shau Valley in two years. The valley, running 35 miles along the western border of Vietnam next to Laos, had been a haven for the enemy since the last Special Forces camp had been abandoned in March 1966.

I still remember Cassius Clay/Muhammad Ali saying, "I ain't got no quarrel with them Viet Cong."

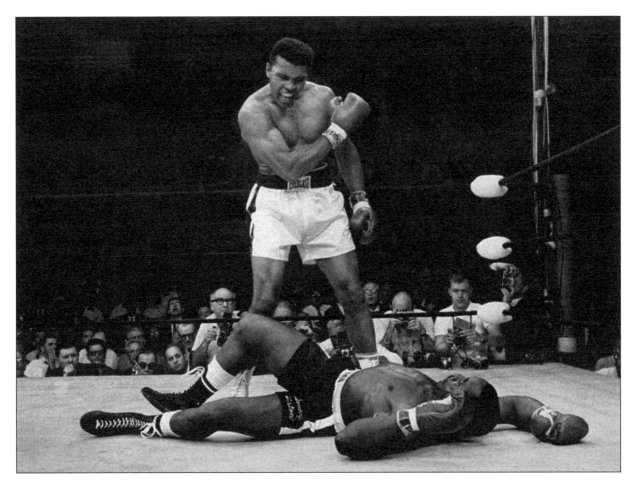

Muhammad Ali vs. Sonny Liston, February 25, 1964, Miami Beach, FL.

This picture shows why it was a good thing for *them* **that Ali** *didn't* **have a "quarrel" with the Viet Cong!**

CHAPTER 3

Behind the "Eight" Ball

During my last term just before graduation in May 1970, Penn State administratively declared that all courses outside of my Business Management major could only be "Pass/Fail." I lost my two "A's" but still finished the term with my "B" in the requisite business management course. *I waited out the draft.* I had a few job interviews, but my student deferment was up and I had no connections to keep me out of the draft.

Events in the U.S. during the half-year leading up to my induction were indicative of a very agitated nation concerning our involvement in Vietnam. I "won" the draft lottery with number "82" early in 1970...so there was a good chance I was going to be *drafted* and that it would be soon after my May 1970 graduation from Penn State.

The Kent State riots protesting the War, and ending in the killing of four students, had shaken up the nation. Even Old Main (the Administration Building at Penn State) was taken over by students during the spring of 1970 to protest the Vietnam War and the Kent State student deaths.

Where, once, it had been thought that "The Woodstock Music Festival" back in 1969 and the afterglow of its message of peace and love—along with the music of Richie Havens, Canned Heat, Janis Joplin, Big Brother and the Holding Company, Jimi Hendrix, and Joe Cocker—was surely going to carry us through to end this Vietnam "side trip" in our nation's destiny, now this belief no longer prevailed.

Janis Joplin
Photograph by Baron Wolman

Jimi Hendrix
Photograph by Baron Wolman

We soon had *Four Dead in Ohio* as Crosby, Stills, Nash, and Young lamented, and my idyllic life in "Happy Valley" (the nickname for the Penn State campus and the "life" and lifestyle it offered), where I was enjoying my Religious Studies and Advanced Philosophy classes during the spring term, was about to turn serious, and I was going to grow up quickly. I had two jobs my senior year at this very large and great public university. I worked in Findlay Dining Hall in East Halls to have an opportunity to better meet the few women who went to Penn State at the time (the ratio was almost three-guys-to-every-female; now it is probably four-girls-to-every-three guys). I also worked as a Campus Patrolman so I could work the art museum, and at Schwab Auditorium to hear nationally recognized speakers like Ralph Abernathy, and watch those home Penn State football games that were usually over by the 3rd quarter.

Then I would put on my hat and shades to direct traffic exiting Beaver Stadium. Penn State used to pull the starters (like Franco Harris and Lydell Mitchell) midway through the 3rd quarter as the game was frequently a rout and a lot of the professional football teams at the time probably could not even stop the Penn State running attack.

I remember writing to my draft board, with a handwritten letter, in July of 1970 asking them to: *"…Get the inevitable over with, as the job market is shaky and I do not think anyone wants to waste their time on hiring and training someone who is already waiting to be drafted."*

The draft lasted only a few years during the Vietnam War (1969-1972) and Gerald Ford ultimately pardoned the draft dodgers in 1974, many of whom fled the country for Canada.

The Vietnam War was an "undeclared" war, that is, not "approved" by the U.S. Congress. This was considered a mere technicality, and we all knew it. It had begun for the U.S. when President Eisenhower sent over military advisors on a small scale to Indochina. The U.S. had just finished up the Korean War and, as the prevailing wisdom went in the State Department, Pentagon, White House, and Congress, we could not afford to lose another country to Communism. (However, Eisenhower was reluctant to commit to direct and full scale intervention unless certain—almost impossible—conditions were met relating to British and southeast Asian participation, U.S. Congressional approval, and continued French participation under American command.)

Our involvement escalated through Presidents Kennedy and Johnson to the point where the U.S. had 475,000 troops in Vietnam by 1967. While attending Penn State from 1966-1970, I was aware of what was reported on television, in magazines, or in the daily newspaper about Vietnam.

I lost one close friend, Dennis Lorenzini from Elizabeth-Forward High School, to the War. "The Beak," as he was nicknamed, was a very good basketball player. He was from Blythdale, PA which was just a few miles from my home. We tried to always be on the same basketball team in P.E. classes. He was a happy guy with a great smile when he was playing ball. I remember his laugh and his gravelly voice.

He served in the Army as an Infantryman with the 2nd Platoon, C Co., 2nd Battalion, 27th Infantry, 25th Infantry Division, and he was killed along with seventeen others in a heavy firefight in Tay Ninh Province in South Vietnam on February 23, 1969.

Sergeant Dennis Lorenzini was awarded the Purple Heart, as he gave his life for his country. Among the other medals awarded him were the Bronze Star, the U.S. Army Commendation Medal, the Vietnam Combat Medal, and the Vietnam Service Medal. He also earned the highly coveted Combat Infantryman Badge.

Dennis Lorenzini's Medals.

The Combat Infantryman Badge.

But I was more fortunate. I had my studies and I never really worried about any Vietnam service for *me*, until I got a "low draft number" in *early 1970!* For years, the stories had been circulating about how boys would go to Canada to avoid the draft, or would fake medical conditions so as to be deemed unfit to serve, or would join the National Guard Reserves if they had a slot in their area, or even try the "Conscientious Objector" route. I never knew what happened to most of the draft eligibles I hung out with, because, as college was coming to an end, I started seriously concentrating on what was going to happen to *me*.

For a long while, I used to think that I lost maybe three to four years of my life to my colleagues in the "business world" after my Penn State graduation with a Bachelor of Science degree, as I had only a two-month waiting period for the draft. Then came my training, my time in Vietnam, and, after discharge, the time when I had to figure out what to do with my future.

But after reliving Vietnam for this book, I can see that I was wrong.

I do not know how I would have coped as a 17-or-18-year old in Vietnam without college. Surely, I would have been in the jungle every day and exposed to more of the horrors of war than what I saw. ...I probably would <u>not</u> have come back alive.

SELECTIVE SERVICE SYSTEM   Approval Not Required.

ORDER TO REPORT FOR
ARMED FORCES PHYSICAL EXAMINATION

TRANSFER BOARD NO. 44
114 N. SPRING STREET
BELLEFONTE, PA. 16823

(Local Board Stamp)

APR 1 3 1970
(Date of mailing)

To

SELECTIVE SERVICE NO.

James M. Cheskawich
411 Pinchot Hall, P. S. U.,
University Park, Pa. 16802

You are hereby directed to present yourself for Armed Forces Physical Examination by reporting
at: South West Main Gate, Beaver
                        Stadium, P. S. U.

(Place of reporting)

on _____ APR 2 7 1970 _____ at __ 5:40 A.M. __ D.S.T.
          (Date)   (Hour)

(Member, Executive Secretary or clerk of Local Board)

**U.S. Army Notice to
Report for Physical Examination.
NOTE the time I was required to be there!**

CHAPTER 4

"Well, You're In the Army Now!"
Basic Training
Ft. Dix, New Jersey
August–October 1970

It was a humid summer evening and the opening two brief sentences coming over the loudspeaker were spoken in the thickest of Texas drawls. "WHY...? VIETNA...M?" The speaker was former President Lyndon Baines Johnson, addressing the new troops and appearing on a large screen in an outdoor amphitheater at Ft. Dix, New Jersey. I had just been drafted the week before and I was now in Basic Training with the U.S. Army.

The War was almost over, wasn't it?...

So *why* was the former President talking about *Vietnam?* I wondered. Why did we have to sit and watch this? We surely were *not* going over *"there,"* since President Nixon had promised the nation to end the War. He had a plan.

Some of us laughed at the thought of being put to the test to see if we were "man enough" to serve in Vietnam.

Maybe I would be going to Germany after Advanced Individual Training (AIT), or maybe I could get a stateside job? I wanted to stay near Pittsburgh, as I was a Pennsylvania country boy at heart and I was certain that with my four-year degree from Penn State in Business, the Army had a good job for me. Still, there were many uncertainties in my mind as to what was going to *happen* to me. How could I let myself get into this predicament? I had left myself vulnerable.

Outside of being thrown together in a common sleeping area with thirty men, there were a few other things that did stand out for me about my Basic Training time. A few weeks into Basic Training, I remember my excitement at my first "G.I. Party"—which turned out to be a cleanup of the living and sleeping quarters with bleach, mops, cleaners of all kind, brooms, etc.! We had a few of these during the eight weeks of Basic Training.

I had only looked forward to the first "party" as I did not know any better. I was really naïve.

As with some of the "characters" at Penn State, a few of the guys in Basic Training were not into personal hygiene. I remember one fellow from the South who used the same unwashed brown towel daily for weeks at a time. We were all issued white towels, but this 17-or 18-year-old's towel was brown by the end of the first week. No wonder he had oversized pimples all over his face! A while later, a few of us destroyed the towel, as it was an eyesore in addition to being a health hazard. Ft. Dix had just gone through a well publicized *influenza outbreak* months before I arrived.

> **We were told, of course, that we had "nothing to**
>
> **worry about." That is <u>also</u> what they told us, too,**
>
> **almost 10,000 miles away and six months later, about**
>
> **the *"Agent Orange"* spraying. "Oh, there is nothing**
>
> **to be concerned about …."**

I soon learned to pace myself in the daily running, as the very first time I ran a timed mile with my boots on, I went way out in front of the group of other runners. I remember the Sergeant saying excitedly over the loudspeaker, "Maybe *this* soldier is going to set a new course record! This is one of the fastest times I have ever seen for half the mile!" Of course, I ran out of gas quickly and had to slow down and walk, as I was breathing very heavily. I completed the rest of the course. You learn these things as you go on. I thought I was fast, but I had never run a mile before that day. Years later, I used to run 5–7 miles a day several days a week, but you have to learn to build up to that kind of mileage.

One early morning toward the end of Basic Training, Drill Sergeant Guzman pulled me out of formation and asked me to take a try at running the troops through the morning drills. I had a high-pitched, squeaky voice when anything came out, but with his coaching, I soon learned to say "Ten Hut" instead of "Attention." Also I learned to say "Fore… Ward… Harch" instead of a quick, "Forward March." Still, I was not Drill Sergeant material and he said so in so many words. He did see "something" in me, though, and I will give him credit.

However, the first time we had "bivouac" (setting up tents for temporary camp sites), he was very upset with us. We were taught how to make our shelter, working with tree limbs or branches, and by tying or snapping our ponchos together. After Midnight, it started to rain and by 1:00 a.m. we were in a downpour with distant lightning and streams of water washing out our carefully constructed sleeping quarters. My three buddies and I decided together, around 2:30 a.m., that we had seen enough rain filling up our shelter and we headed for cover in the nearest building.

We found the latrine, but so had about forty other guys. We sat on the floor for a while with our backs against the wall and tried to get some sleep. The Sergeant found us all around 3:00 a.m. and gave us a verbal thrashing. He told us that we were *not* "men," yet, and would not survive in a war zone because we were "weak." I wondered *why* he was referring to a *"war zone…."*

By 5:30 a.m. the rain stopped and we discovered that only three men had stayed in-place outside, under their ponchos, as they were on higher terrain and did not get washed out with the flooding.

You make your choices and you have to pay the penalty when caught for making a bad choice. The vast majority of the group (minus the three) had to get up at 3:00 a.m. back in the barracks the next day and get to work on a cleanup detail as punishment. Although he told us of our early wake up call, not one of us seriously believed the Sergeant was going to be up that early. He seemed to enjoy waking us from our sleep and put us to work quickly on another "G.I. Party." Breakfast at the Mess Hall was still many hours away.

I am still not sure why the Second Lieutenants constantly waited hidden behind bushes as we exited from the Mess Hall all during Basic. They were just a nuisance and we ended up despising them rather than respecting them for their rank. After doing the requisite twenty or thirty push-ups to appease the "offended" officer for not saluting, I caught on to the game and slowed down my rush to exit the Mess Hall so I would not be caught off guard to my surroundings. My thought on Second Lieutenants was I just did *not* want to *be* one, as the "scuttlebutt" was that they had to lead the ambush patrols in Vietnam and were the *first* to get shot by the enemy.

You hear a lot of rumors and gossip in the Army and it is impossible to know the truth from a fabricated story designed to impress or just pass the time. I had not seen anything like the Army's rumor mill while back at Penn State. But I was getting educated to the real world now that I was in the Army.

I remember very clearly an obnoxious team leader who was a Specialist 4th Class who started verbally pushing us around in the barracks. He was just *mean*. The Drill Sergeant caught him in some weekend infraction about half-way through Basic Training and "busted him" to a PV-1, which was our entry grade into the Army! The man really could have played the running back position in tackle football, and, like Jim Brown, it usually took five guys to bring him down. But we did not feel sorry that he got disciplined, as it dented his ego and he was more *humane* around us during the rest of Basic Training. We even learned to like and respect the "reformed" man.

I also remember the time my buddy Frank Champ (from River Hill, near Monongahela, PA) and I worked together to double tackle him in a pick-up football game. Frank told me of his plan. He hit him low and I hit him high and we brought him down. The man was good and should have been playing ball somewhere, we thought. Frank was pretty good in his own right.

My buddy, Frank Champ.

He was a year ahead of me in high school, a quiet, solid, studious individual. I thought that it was great that we ended up at Boot Camp together.

New Jersey in the heat of summer is not an ideal place to be playing soldier, but the Army was "toughening us up" and "making men" out of us. One of my other friends from near my hometown was in "Sick Bay" for most of Basic Training as he had a stress fracture in his foot and could not do the running in the morning. Of course, a lot of guys thought he was faking it as we had not seen the X-rays, and we let him know what we thought of his apparent malingering. He eventually was soon medically discharged as "useless" to the Army.

I bulked up nearly ten pounds in Basic from good food and hard work. I learned to make a bed with a green Army blanket tight enough to bounce a dime, and finally mastered the art of spit-shining those black boots. I even learned how to enjoy Kitchen Police ("KP") more, as one day "a brother" and I split a 6-pack of *Colt 45 Mustang Malt Liquor* while running outside to scrub the pots and sip beer. Well, maybe it was two 6-packs....

Diana Ross was singing over the radio *Ain't No Mountain High Enough* (with the Funk Brothers playing in the studio orchestra, but we didn't know this at the time), and we thought we were doing pretty well if we could enjoy KP this way in the heat of a New Jersey summer. I only was assigned KP two to three times during Basic. Often it was used as punishment on top of a regular rotational assignment that everyone had to perform.

Had I been caught with the beer, I could have been given KP for a month. What kind of story would I have had to make up to tell Mom? That was probably the hardest part.

I was 22-years-old when I finished Basic Training and feeling pretty good about this new stage in my life. I had "qualified" with the M-16 and in throwing grenades. I was fast and I could go up and down a rope pretty quickly. No more studying late at night, no more "Blue Books," no more worrying about how many classes can I cut and still get a "B" in the course, etc. The Army was taking care of everything for me and I found Basic to be easy.

At this point, we had not been told where we were going to be sent for our Advanced

Individual Training (AIT), *and I certainly did not think I would need any special combat training as I was never going to Vietnam!*

I still had grand wishes of going to Germany, or even staying stateside for my two-year commitment. Germany could have been a lot of fun. Draftees served twenty-four months at the time. (During World War II, the service obligation was longer.)

My feeling was: "When you are called, you serve, and you do not gripe about it."

But I always tried to stay ahead of the Army's "game plan" for me.

Issuance of the M-16.

CHAPTER 5

Advanced Individual Training Camp (AIT)

Fort Ord, CA
Fall 1970

I was ready for Advanced Individual Training (AIT) at Fort Ord, California just as The Carpenters sang with their smash hit that had come out in the late summer, *We've Only Just Begun.*

But there was a *disconnect* between Karen Carpenter's sweet, angelic voice and the harsh realities coming up over the horizon of a new year. I also remember *It's A Shame* by The Spinners in the Summer/Fall of Basic Training and that was a better song to relate to for those of us who had just been drafted, as we did not have grandiose dreams of glory for the months ahead. We weren't planning on Vietnam as we did not look that far ahead…the Army did all the planning for you!

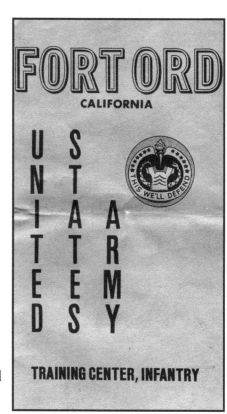

On the play list on the next page, these songs were popular not only in the Army and Air Force training camps but also all around the country.

◄ The arrow is added to indicate especially remembered songs.

ARMY AIR FORCE EXCHANGE SERVICE

TOP 50 POPS

November 2, 1970

INV	LW	TW	BUC	
	8	1	I Think I Love You	Partridge Family
	6	2	Fire & Rain	James Taylor
	1	3	We've Only Just Begun ◄	The Carpenters
	10	4	Express Yourself	Watts 103rd St. Band
	2	5	All Right Now	Free
	14	6	Somebody's Been Sleeping	One Hundred Proof
	4	7	Lola	The Kinks
	16	8	Indiana Wants Me	R. Dean Taylor
	3	9	I'll Be There	Jackson Five
	18	10	Gypsy Woman	Brian Hyland
	5	11	Cracklin' Rosie	Neil Diamond
	20	12	Engine #9	Wilson Pickett
	7	13	Green Eyed Lady	Sugar Loaf
	41	14	Tears Of A Clown	Smokey Robinson
	12	15	God, Love, and Rock & Roll	Teagarden & Van Winkle
	28	16	Yellow River	Christie
	9	17	Out In The Country	Three Dog Night
	24	18	Deeper, Deeper	Freda Payne
	11	19	It's Only Make Believe	Glen Campbell
	32	20	Let's Work Together	Canned Heat
	13	21	Groovy Situation	Gene Chandler
	34	22	Make It Easy On Yourself	Dionne Warwick
	15	23	That's Where I Went Wrong	Poppy Family
	36	24	See Me, Feel Me	The Who
	17	25	It's A Shame ◄	The Spinners
	39	26	Cry Me A River	Joe Cocker
	19	27	Julie, Do You Love Me	Bobby Sherman
	48	28	No Matter What	Bad Finger
	22	29	El Condor Pasa	Simon & Garfunkel
	49	30	Heed The Call	Kenny Rogers
	30	31	Lucretia MacEvil	Blood, Sweat & Tears
	40	32	It Don't Matter To Me	Bread
	21	33	Our House	Crosby, Stills, Nash..
	44	34	After Midnight	Eric Clapton
	26	35	Do What You Wanna Do	Five Flights Up
	45	36	Still Waters	Four Tops
	23	37	Ain't No Mountain High Enough ◄	Diana Ross
	46	38	Poquito Soul	One G Plus Three
	25	39	Long, Long Time	Linda Ronstadt
	47	40	Montego Bay	Bobby Bloom
	27	41	Look What They've Done To My Song	New Seekers
	42	42	Closer To Home	Grand Funk
	29	43	Candida	Dawn
	DB	44	You Don't Have To Say You Love Me	Elvis Presley
	33	45	Patches	Clarence Carter
	DB	46	Domino	Van Morrison
	37	47	War ◄	Edwin Starr
	DB	48	Stand By Your Man	Candi Staton
	50	49	Share The Land	Guess Who
	DB	50	He Ain't Heavy ◄	Neil Diamond

At the time, it did not make any sense to me that I was ordered to go to Fort Ord, California to be trained as an *"Infantryman."* I wanted to stay at Ft. Dix since it was close to home, but "Uncle Sam" knows best. Later I heard that the terrain and climate around Fort Ord were considered to most approximate the *jungle* . . . but, even then, we didn't have any place like Vietnam in the U.S.

I do remember being told that we most definitely were *not* going to Vietnam during most of the Advanced Individual Training (AIT) and that we had *"nothing to worry about."*

I believed this to be true, so I enjoyed sunny California in October and November when Jim Plunkett was leading Stanford University, and as I started to be more aware of the ramifications of the choices I was making. In the dorm at Penn State, you might try to be friends with everyone. Here in the Army, I became more selective of my friends and started looking more for common values and interests. I did not need to be playing cards or craps for money. I watched the games but had no interest in taking someone else's money because I already knew I could play Pinochle pretty well and had seen what I could do in accounting courses with minimal studying. I had my skills and tried not to show up anyone.

I made good friends with a very quiet Native American who happened to be very level-headed and was by far the strongest soldier in our company. He did not drink, party, or goof-off. Some of the other guys seemed to have a little thing going with drugs or drinking and I wanted to keep my distance. I was 22-years-old, with a degree, and I was in a group with a lot of 18- and 19-year-old young men.

During one weekend, three weeks into AIT, about five or six of the guys wanted to go to San Francisco to party. The Drill Sergeant told us that we could stay around or only go into Castroville two miles away but, even then, he was not giving out any passes longer than one day. My Native American friend and I were the only two left in the barracks that day as everyone else cleared out quickly. We walked around the base, talked, read, and had our own quiet time. The contingent of boys that went to San Francisco on Saturday never showed up until Monday morning. I could not believe it! The Sergeant showed no leniency, as the boys admitted to going to San Francisco and somehow he found out marijuana was involved. I cannot remember what he did to them but he probably bounced them back to Private, E-1. I think they also lost all "Leave" privileges for the rest of AIT. They may not have even graduated with the rest of us on time.

I was glad I did not join the small group, and this *reinforced* in me that *I just cannot do what my peer group wants to do,* as *I am responsible for myself.*

This lesson stayed with me: I do tell the kids in school where I substitute teach that you make your choices and you have to "own up" to being responsible for your choices. You cannot let your peers drag you down.

This was just the beginning of many times when I would go off to be on my own and not do what the crowd was doing. It had "high survival" value for me—given my independent streak.

Later on, when we could travel farther, during one of the weekends my friend Andy from high school and I visited Salinas and Castroville, enjoying close proximity to the water, the October sunshine, and finally dressing in civilian clothes after wearing Fatigues for weeks at Fort Ord. We also visited Monterey, which was the source, inspiration, or setting for many of John Steinbeck's stories.

Something about Steinbeck had always stuck with me and I imagined what it would be like to write something like *Cannery Row, Grapes of Wrath,* or *Of Mice and Men.* This had to be the first time I even thought of writing! I could fill up a "Blue Book" at Penn State quickly, but there was no time, then, for editing or research which I believed critical to the writing process.

I was not ready to be a writer at the time, as I think one should "live first" to get balance and perspective. This was especially so of a Business major with a lot of rough edges, whose favorite class in high school was physical education.

**A high school friend,
Andy Sedlak.**

However, physical education did take an upper hand. As AIT moved into the last few weeks, I found myself volunteering for certain events as a "Tester" or "Dummy." This was a good sign. I was more sure of myself, and in what I could do, including making me *fearless in handling a weapon or in hand-to-hand combat.*

It demonstrated that the Army training had made me grow in confidence of my capabilities.

I also volunteered to demonstrate the "new, light, anti-tank weapon" that was called "LAW." There was a back blast area that you had to be careful about or you could lose a limb or kill another soldier who was too close. Before firing, the Sergeant had me re-position myself so I didn't lose my leg from the back blast … and I *successfully* hit the tank and watched it go up in flames!

Another time, I heard my voice volunteering to *rappel 200-feet down* a vertical cliff that had been specially chiseled away so that the descent was pretty clean. It was, supposedly, to give us "training" to *jump from a helicopter, without a parachute!* In the Army, the advice from those barrack's experts in the know is that: *"You never volunteer!"* For me, during AIT and later in Vietnam, I found this to be too restrictive and I wanted the chance at excitement and probably glory! I did not want to sit back and miss something! But, as I gradually learned, you have to be selective and use your intelligence.

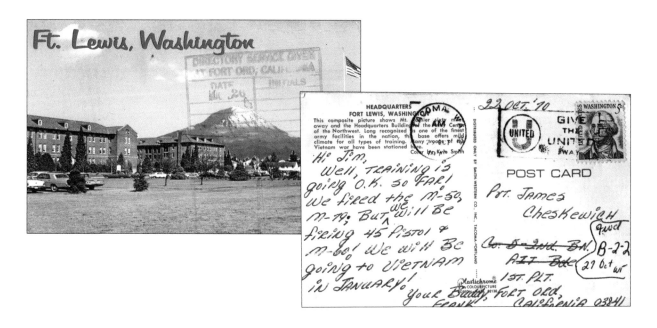

As we approached the last two weeks of AIT, we anxiously awaited our destination for assignment. One night, an office boy working just a few hours a week in the Headquarters Office leaked the news to all of us. At first we thought it was just another one of those "rumors" that guys cook up to get everyone worked up. However, the clerk insisted that "most of us were going to Vietnam," as he had seen the orders or Manifest in writing. I was now coming way too close to what Frank and others already knew. Then, one day after formation, the Captain reported the following:

> **"Men, it is my duty to inform you that the orders for this unit have *changed* over the last few days. I am sorry to relay the news to you that *you are going to be sent over as fully trained Infantrymen to fight in the Vietnam War.***
>
> **I know that you are ready, and I know that you will be tough soldiers…because you are the best trained in the world."**

The majority of us were told to report in a few weeks to Oakland, California, for deployment to South Vietnam.

All I could think about for a few days was: *How could this happen?*

I was going to Vietnam!

This was not in my personal life plan and, as the folks say now-a-days, it wasn't on my "Bucket List."

(Very) Brief Interlude

December 1970

**Remembering my family, the day I left for the War:
my brother Bernie (age 20) in the back,
and left to right, my brother Larry (age 15),
my sister Colleen (age 17),
my Mom, and me.**

CHAPTER 6

"Farewell...."

I returned home for about three weeks of furlough before I had to report to Oakland, California late in December 1970 for a flight to South Vietnam. I remember visiting close friends and relatives, trying to relax and do *something... anything* to take my mind off where I was going and my destiny—whatever that was going to be. I remember going to a few nightclubs in the Pittsburgh area and dancing a little, as I was not sure I would return. I was not a great dancer but I forced myself to get out on the dance floor after finding a partner. I was not dating anyone at the time so I had to toughen up and get used to a lot of rejections of requests to just dance.

No one knows their fate when you have orders to report for transport to a war.

You pray, try to stay out of trouble, pray some more, but I was not capable of relaxing.

I remember seeing Frank Champ's wife in St. Michael's Roman Catholic Church. She kissed me on the cheek after Mass one Sunday and asked me to send her love to her husband, Frank, if I ran into him over in Vietnam. Frank had already gone over, as we were separated after Basic and went to different bases for AIT.

The day arrived when I had to go off to war.

I took less than an hour to pack after church, making sure to take a rosary, a pocket-sized *New Testament*, two black-and-white, small pictures of my family, and Norman Vincent Peale's *The Power of Positive Thinking*. The Sergeant at Fort Ord had instructed us not to bring anything except two to three days of clothing and some personal hygiene products, but we were probably going to have to leave most of that behind anyway at some point as, if it was not "government issued," we probably could not have it in a war.

I packed quickly, and with sadness, as I listened to WAMO-FM and Porky Chedwick probably for the last time on my Allied Component stereo receiver. (I had thought many times

Rhythm n' Blues 860 AM

DOUBLE WAMO

Rhythm n' Blues 106 FM

SUPERSURVEY

PITTSBURGH'S ONLY AUTHENTIC RHYTHM & BLUES RECORD SURVEY

THE TERRIBLE TEN

SEPTEMBER 8 THRU SEPTEMBER 14

	Title	Artist	Label
1.	TELL HIM	PATTI DREW	CAPITOL
2.	GET ON UP	ESQUIRES	BUNKY
3.	MEMPHIS SOUL STEW	KING CURTIS	ATCO
4.	MY EVERYTHING/ FLIP	TEMPTATIONS	GORDY
5.	SOUL MAN	SAM & DAVE	ATLANTIC
6.	THE REAL THING	ERNIE K. DOE	DUKE
7.	YOUR PRECIOUS LOVE	MARVIN & TAMMI	TAMLA
8.	I WANNA TESTIFY	THE PARLIMENTS	REVILOT
9.	CROSS MY HEART	BILLY STEWART	CHESS
10.	BABY I LOVE YOU	ARETHA FRANKLIN	ATLANTIC

THE DOUBLE WAMO SUPERSTARS

SIR WALTER

THE SUPER HITS

* AIN'T NO BIG THING-Electrons Shock
* EVERYDAY OF MY LIFE-Augustine Twins - Duke
* STEREO FREEZE-Stereo's - Hyde
* YOU'VE GOT TO PAY-Al Kent - Ric Tic
* I'M A DRIFTER-Lowell Fulsom - Kent
* ODE TO BILLY JOE-King Pins-Atco
* FUNKY BROADWAY-Wilson Picket - Atlantic
* LET'S BUGALOO-Magics - R.F.A.
* SPREADING HONEY-103st. Rythum Band - Keymen
* I'M A FOOL FOR YOU-James Carr - Goldwax
I'M AFRAID-Lovettes - Carnival
I'M SO LONELY-Intruders -Gamble
KNOCK ON WOOD-Ottis & Carla - Stax
COLD SWEAT-James Brown - King
KARATE BOO GA LOO-Jerry O-Shout
TAKE A LOOK-Aretha Franklin - Columbia
LET THEM TALK-Witches & Warlock Sew City
I NEED YOU-Curtis Blamdon -Tower
TELLING IT LIKE IT IS-Miller Sisters - GMC

HOW STRONG MY LOVE IS- Sweet Inspirations - Atlantic
FUNKY DONKEY-Pretty Purdie - Date
IT'S TOO LATE-Toni Lamarr - Kama Sutra
TALKING ABOUT MY MAN-Mary Love - Modern
MEAN & BROKENHEARTED-Masterkeys Sport
SO THIS IS LOVE-Tommy Mosley-ERA
BEYOND MY FINGERTIPS-Loveables- Toot
GIVING UP YOUR LOVE-Twentie Grans Columbia
I FEEL GOOD-Jean Wells - Calla
MISSING YOU-Luther Ingran - KoKo
YOU KEEP RUNNING AWAY-4 Top's - Motown
TEARS OF JOY-Vicki Anderson-King
O-O I LOVE YOU-Dells - Cadet
SHOUT BAMALAMA-Mickey Murray-S.S.S.
WHAT'VE I DONE TO MAKE YOU MAD-Linda Jones - Loma
OOH BABY YOU TURN ME ON-Willie Mitchell Hi
HEART BE STILL-Lorraine Ellison - Loma

HAL BROWN

PORKY CHEDWIC

BROTHER MATT

RUN JOE - FREDDIE SCOTT - SHOUT

Double WAMO SHOWSTOPPER

BILL POWELL

that this was going to be "it" and there would be no more Roberto Clemente, Willie Stargell, WMCK and Terry Lee, Motown, Bob Prince, Joe Tucker, and St. Michael's Church, as this could be the end.)

WAMO-AM & FM was Pittsburgh's first Black-owned radio station and also one of the first in a large U. S. market. For many years, WAMO had one of the strongest signals of any FM radio station in southwestern Pennsylvania. I particularly liked its "blend" of R & B (rhythm and blues) music.

My brother Bernie drove me to the Greater Pittsburgh airport. The Steelers were having another losing season anyway, so I thought I might as well skip town. But this new guy named Terry Bradshaw could be a player.

It was a short flight to Oakland in my dress uniform, and I remember looking out the airplane window and seeing my reflection.

I almost saw the tears on my face, but I quickly wiped them away.

After a day or two in Oakland, California—and after a short telephone call to my Mom with her admonition to *"Be careful around those girls over there…"* (But I was thinking, "Hey, what about the *VC,* Mom?")—I was off on a long plane ride to somewhere around Saigon.

I am sure I had a few more tears, and I still had a headache from the late night partying the evening before I left home. (I had downed **19**…and, yes, they were *counted!*…"Singapore Slings.") I think we stopped in Anchorage, Alaska on the way. I remember that I sat up front in the plane next to a One or Two-Star General for part of the trip.

I thought about what I left behind…and what I needed to do in Vietnam to *survive*.

Looking out the window, and wondering…

PART TWO

"In-Country" with
The 101st Airborne Division:
"The Eagle Has Landed"

Of all the units to end up with, I had the good fortune to end up with *the best!*

The 101st has a legendary past, having distinguished itself in the Battle of the Bulge, Normandy, and Alsace in World War II, and later on "Hamburger Hill" in Vietnam.

It was a source of pride to serve with them as the 101st Airborne Division is one of this country's most highly decorated fighting units.

Upon its arrival in South Vietnam in 1965, it was called an "Airborne Unit." In 1968, the unit was re-designated "Airmobile," as the unit entered battles in Vietnam by helicopter. That is why I was trained to rappel. In 1974, the unit became identified as "Air Assault," but I was long gone by then.

It was reported that the North Vietnamese feared *"The Chicken Men"* as the "Screaming Eagles" were often referred to by the enemy!

In researching material for this book, I came across a reference to the killed-and-wounded-in-action totals from the 101st Airborne Division in Vietnam.

We had over 20,000 soldiers killed or wounded in action. We were in some of the bloodiest battles.

CHAPTER 7

Welcome to The War!

We landed at Bien Hoa/Long Binh airfield which was just outside Saigon. I remember the overpowering and thick smell of diesel fumes and the humid air as soon as we exited from the plane. We were taken by an open cattle truck to temporary quarters to last no more than one or two nights until we received our permanent assignment which would be somewhere in Vietnam. The first night was extremely noisy and I do not remember sleeping. We had rocket and mortar attacks all night in the vicinity. It sounded like 25-feet away and I remember diving under the sleeping cot for cover several times.

I was not going to die on my first day in "Nam!"

Loud screams and the movement of heavy equipment pierced the night. Around 2:00 a.m., someone came into our sleeping quarters and shouted out a call for "blood donors." I did not have the Type they needed critically so I didn't have to volunteer so quickly. I would get more opportunities to volunteer later in Vietnam.

We had not received our M-16 rifles yet and we were told to stay put and not wander around. I was not going to argue. It seemed like a lot of Army personnel people were barking out orders and there was a constant stream of soldiers and locals milling around. It was warm. I could not stop the perspiration, and the burning diesel smell was not dissipating. I wanted to stay alive so I did exactly as I was told.

I could hear pretty well, back then, so I am sure I did not need a repeat of any explanation.

A short time later, someone in charge of relaying information said that I was going by a C-130 plane to "I Corps" at Da Nang and then on to Phu Bai by *cattle truck* to serve with the 101st Airborne Division and…why wasn't I on that plane? That's the way the Army operated: "Hurry up and wait …" or, "You best be moving, soldier, as you are late!" I was not paid to think, so I ran to the plane and caught my flight. We were strapped and buckled in, and I half expected to be told we had to hook up the parachutes for a jump, but they had not trained me to use a parachute. They packed us in tightly.

At some point, I was put on a helicopter with others and dropped off in the rice paddies so that I only had to jump two-to-four feet without a parachute. I just had to land successfully without breaking my legs and I think I may have gone down the rope first. In any case, we were trained to rappel and I landed successfully. Most of the skill is with the helicopter pilot who selects where to drop you. If there is enemy fire, you may get dropped off where you have more "air time" but you are not getting a parachute and so you "hit, tuck, and roll."

Many years later when I rode horses and was thrown or jumped off, the training had obviously taken hold permanently as I never broke a bone coming off a galloping horse. However, I would not recommend that anyone except professionals try this. It is amazing what you learn in the Army.

We were highly trained; of that, I had no doubt while I served with them. The 101st also had me now, as the Army had built up my confidence level to *fight*. I was fast, strong, smart,

kept my own counsel, followed orders, and I did not have the overdeveloped ego to stand out and get shot at first—by friendly fire or the enemy. I was painfully shy (and that had started long ago, around 4th grade for me) and I struggled and worked hard to deal with it.

I wanted to be a model soldier.

On His Blindness

"When I consider how my light is spent

E're half my days, in this dark world and wide,

And that one talent which is death to hide

Lodg'd with me useless, though my soul more bent

To serve therewith my Maker, and present

My true account, least he be returning chide,

Doth God exact day-labour, light deny'd,

I fondly ask; but patience to prevent

That murmur, soon replies, God doth not need

Either man's work or his own gifts, who best

Bear his milde yoak, they serve him best, his State

Is Kingly. Thousands at his bidding speed

And post o're Land and Ocean without rest:

They also serve who only stand and waite."

John Milton, 1655

CHAPTER 8

"How Did This Happen?"

Camp Campbell
Phu Bai, Vietnam
January 1971

The first few days at Phu Bai—which was about 30-miles south of the "Demilitarized Zone" (DMZ) separating North and South Vietnam—were devoted to processing-in and some more weapons training. At some point early, I was issued my own M-16 and cartridges, along with Jungle Fatigues, and was told to wait for further orders.

I still could not believe that I was in Vietnam! I woke up early one morning in my cot with a thin mattress and realized the bed was *wet*....

I kept my mouth shut, as even if guys were playing tricks on other guys as at Penn State with shaving cream games under the room doors and salt in the bed, it is better to just keep quiet. Of course, I was nervous and unsure of what was going to happen to me, but I did not admit it to anyone. None of us did.

The M-16 long-distance training was to make sure that we could see accurately and how often you could hit the target, which was 400 yards away (which equates to almost 366 meters, or longer than two back-to-back and strung-out Mickey Mantle home runs). You have to adjust the scope. My qualifying score was only as a Marksman back in Basic Training, which was only at 25 meters away with the M-16. I thought it was impossible for me to get a decent score at 400 yards away but AIT had improved my skills and there is nothing like fear in a *war zone* to make you truly focused. The Sergeant on the firing line helped me make quick adjustments for wind and I hit the target 17-out-of-20 shots. The Army would not have sent me over if I was not ready. But, with a score like that, I *could qualify* to be a sniper...and sent out to combat!

"... Operation Hawthorne ... the classic spoiler ..."

".. The battle raged on ..."

"... The brigade found a home-of sorts ..."

and Combat...

tion **Hawthorne** became the classic spoiling attack as it blunted the NVA offensive in Kontum Province.

The "Above the Rest" and "Strike Force" troopers unloaded from their C-130s at Dak To and looked around them. They were in the beautiful green jungle of the cool highlands, but as they looked to the left and right, then in front and rear, they saw a ring of mountains all around them, and behind those even taller jungled mountains. "I've never seen Dien Bien Phu," said one trooper, "but this sure looks like the description."

It was one of the most viciously contested battles of the Vietnam War. Once the battle was joined, the fighting was continuous. Day and night the battle raged, moving from bunker to trench line, to spider hole, to bamboo thicket, to stream bed—and finally,

to victory. In a brilliant scheme of maneuver, the two Screaming Eagle battalions executed a double envelopment against the entrenched 24th NVA Regt.—the 1st of the 327th attacking north and the 2nd of the 502nd attacking south. All this was supported by massive fire-power including artillery (27,000 rounds) and bombs (473 Air Force sorties).

At the end of **Hawthorne**, the 24th NVA Regt. had been destroyed—it suffered more than 1,200 dead—and the offensive stopped dead in its tracks. Lt. Gen. Stanley R. Larsen, then commanding general of I Field Force, publicly stated that the 1st Brigade was the "best fighting unit in Vietnam."

Operation Wheeler started Sept. 11, 1967, near Chu Lai. Continuing under Task Force Oregon—which was redesignated the Americal Division—the Screaming Eagles encountered elements of the 2nd NVA Division west of Tam Ky.

Surprise airmobile assaults into the Song Tranh Valley flushed out the enemy. Paratroopers killed scores of the fleeing NVA. After three weeks enemy dead had risen to 396, and by early November to more than 800, making **Wheeler** the largest single operation conducted by the brigade in Vietnam.

Pfc. William Austin was leading his squad of Co A., 2nd Bn., 502nd Abn. Inf., across a rice paddy near Chu Lai when a water buffalo charged from some bushes. Everybody beat a retreat except Austin, who stood rooted to the spot. He sidestepped and thrust his M-16

CHAPTER 9

Posted

_____

One evening, I was at the Enlisted Men's Club with my friend from New England whom I will call "Ike." It was getting close to 2:00 a.m. and he said he had to go get some sleep because he had to get up early the next day and take a "typing test." I laughed when I heard this, as I knew all about these Army rumors and stories.

He continued to tell me, "Look, if you have a Bachelor's Degree and can type, they could use hard-working college graduates in the Personnel Branch of the 101st Airborne Division at Camp Campbell."

"I did not have to type too much in college as I always paid someone else to type my term papers," I told Ike. "I don't think I am a good-enough typist, but anything is better than going out in the jungle with a ruck-sack and rifle to look for Commies!" (Well, maybe the only thing worse was having them look for me.)

We had one more round of drinks, which I bought in gratitude for the tip about the typing exam, and I showed up with Ike the next morning at 5:30 a.m. to meet the E-7 or E-8 Sergeant who was giving the test. He took our names and told the boys from the middle to the back of the line that he could only test so many. For those in the front of the line, he told us to get a good breakfast and be back by 7:00 a.m.

I took the typing test and fortunately we had to type *The Declaration of Independence,* of which I knew most of the words, without having to look down at the words on paper. I used one and sometimes two fingers and typed as fast as I could, sweating through my Fatigues and feeling the beads of sweat developing on my forehead. I typed faster than Gregory Peck who played a former World War II Captain tasked with typing-out his autobiography for a job interview in *The Man in the Gray Flannel Suit*, but I knew I was out of my element. We were told to stop. That seemed to be almost right after just beginning the test! I turned over the completed work and anxiously waited for a few minutes. It did not take long.

The Sergeant went out of the room and then re-appeared and said I had a new job as a "Personnel Clerk," if I wanted the job! I had passed the test with 23-words-a-minute and 3-errors which gave me the bare minimum of 20-words-a-minute. I think he was laughing because he knew the magnitude of the test results. I accepted my new job without any hesitation, let out a yell, and knew I was fortunate, indeed. I was not as fortunate as the *Fortunate Son* by Creedence Clearwater Revival, who was born with a silver spoon in his mouth, but I was in luck!

I was determined that over time I was going to be a much better typist but, unfortunately, I never really got any better with the manual model typewriter. I had reached my level of incompetency as a typist. By my own assessment, I was horrible as a typist and always worried the Army would find out that I was an imposter. I used to practice typing during my lunch half-hour but always hid that typing practice when anyone came close to my desk. I never could finish a full page, though I tried many times.

In retrospect, I suppose I was an embarrassment to all the soldiers who really could type. I did not deserve to have "Typing" next to my "Personnel Clerk" designation as my "Duty Military Occupational Specialty." But the alternative, as a "Primary Trained Infantryman" who could hit a target pretty often from 400 yards away, was probably going to get me killed.

I could *shoot* better than *type*, but being a typist for the rest of my tour was probably going to get me home alive. I soon discovered, as did my Team Leader, that I had other critical administrative and bookkeeping skills that would prove my worth to the 101st Administrative Company.

When I started my year, I was optimistic, energetic, and trying to make the best of a difficult situation. It is a good plan to rotate men throughout a war, as fresh soldiers are always coming in and soldiers can plan on leaving by a certain date.

Most do make it, but the cost of war is very high.... I was quickly introduced to the "Short Timer's Calendar," where a soldier can color-in a block for each of the "Last 100 Days" to stay alive. There were many variations, and most were filled out for the "Last 10 Days."

I also noticed very early on that some of the soldiers greeted each other with "The Dap," which is a modified handshake involving a series of finger and hand movements and clasping fingers and closed fists. There were variations, and sometimes you had to know what the pattern was in order to finish the ritual correctly. I tried it a few times but never really got that good at it. I saw more of this type of greeting after the War than during undergraduate school at Penn State. I am not sure where it started but it seemed to enhance the *bonding* that *reinforced* we were in this *together* and we would work as a unit, not as individuals looking for glory or trying to stand out.

Often the guys would show the "Peace Sign" to each other, which involves the index and middle finger on one hand in the shape of a "V." This, even I could do.

Phu Bai was the Headquarters for the 101st Airborne Division in "I-Corps" South Vietnam. We had a lot of paperwork to do in the 101st Administrative Company. I remember some of our fellow soldiers referring to the 101st Administrative Company as the *"101st Chairborne Division."* Some of the guys laughingly called it the *"One-Oh-Worst-Division,"* but we knew we were anything but that.

We were proud to be in the 101st!

Three members of our Personnel Unit absorbed in paperwork
and communication relays with other Units.

But…we also knew that we would not have been laughing…if we had to go out and fight every day.

4/5/71

Hi Jim,

    I very sorry for not writing sooner but I have been very busy
down here at DaNang. I am working with Headquarters, Headquarters Company
under the 212TH. Combat Aviation Battalion*** I was very lucky to keep
from going into the field as a Grunt*** My Electronics Background helped
a lot*** I was to be the unit's radio dispatcher but you had to be a
E-4 or higher to get the position; so I was placed with Headquarters
working with IRO (Vietnamese - Local Nationalists). I may later get the
radio dispatcher position--- I'll have to wait and see***

    Ps: We have been getting hit quite often here at the 212TH. with
        rockets & mortars** Some have hit pretty close to my hootch***
    (Within 300m) A couple of times***

    I hope everything is going well with you***
    In case you don't know Lucas is a father of a bouncing baby boy***

                His address:

                          (In case you want to write to him***)

        Address:

            PFC. Lenford L. Lucas
            ████████████
            23d. Admin. Co. (Cas. Br.)
            23d. Infantry Division
            APO S.F.   96374

        Ps: Hope to hear from you, and I will be answering your
            letters now***

                                        Your Buddy,

                                        Frank

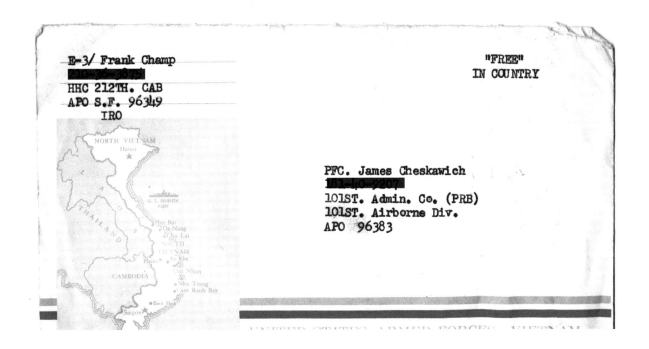

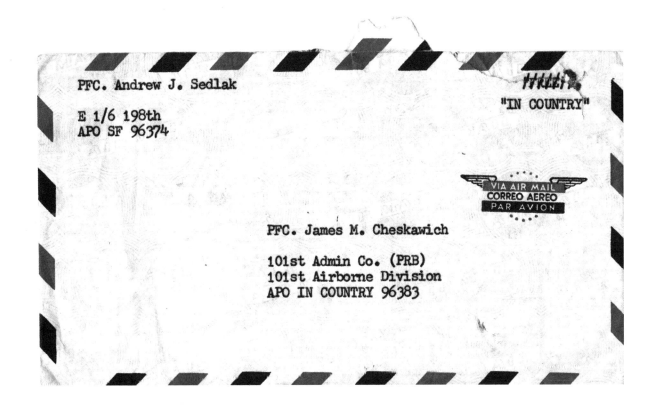

21 March 71

Hi,

    As you have probably quessed from the type written letter I am no longer in the field.

    I answered your first letter but it was returned with "No Record" stamped on it. So I'll try again. Hopefully they will get this one to you.

    I quess I'll fill you in on what has happened so far.

    First of all upon arriving in the country I got sent to /Chu Lai. I lucked out and was placed in amortar company. I really had it easy. All we did was sit around our little LZ and occasionally fire a mission. Of course we had to fore go a few conviences. Like taking showers and having hot chow.

    After about two weeks in the field I got sent on a special trip to Da Nang. There I was a security quard for two weeks at ahospital. (please exscuse all these typing errors as I am not a typist) The whole two weeks was like being on vacation. The only bad thing about it was that there was so many things to do that I spent quite a bit of money. That trip ended around February 15. Then I returned to my mortar location. After Being out there approximately a month I got a chance at this rear job. I really did not want to take it. But my family and girl worry so much I figured it would make them feel better. But I have the option that if they hassle me too much I can go back to the field.

    THat brings me up to the present, where I am now the mail clerk for our company. It's not a bad job but I now do more work than when I was out in the field. However, I don't pull KP or qurad or any other type of details. I've got my own job and that's it. If I had to do all the extra duties you pull I would definitely be back in the field.

    Being in the field is much different than what you probably imagine it to be. I really enjoyed it out there. But there is no way I would want to take the place of those guys that have to hump.

    I quess that covers everything for now. I hope this letter gets to you this time.

PEACE,

CHAPTER 10

The First Days

When I started my tour with the 101st in the Personnel Branch, it was still early January 1971. I remember listening to the Super Bowl in the afternoon over a small radio someone had turned on that was nearby the outside ice cream stand where I bought my first *"yellow-brown vanilla ice cream cone."*

I did not know if we were hearing a delayed broadcast, or the live game, over the Armed Forces Radio network. The game was played January 17, 1971 and Baltimore beat Dallas 16-13 with Johnny Unitas throwing a touchdown pass. I thought at the time that this cannot be too bad—being in a war zone listening to Unitas beat "America's team." The Steelers were still a few years away from being a legitimate Play-Off team, so I had to root for "Johnny U" who was born in Pittsburgh and had been cut by the Steelers in 1955 as not being "smart enough" to be a NFL quarterback!

Our "office" was a large building that could probably house a modern-day Boeing 747 airplane. It was sectioned off for the different units and teams, but it was an "open air" building with a slanted roof set on top of a rectangular box. The walls were made of corrugated aluminum.

There was nothing fancy about it and, of course, there was no central heating or cooling system.

**Eating lunch in front of
the Administration "building."**

There was a helicopter launching and landing pad that was about *25-feet behind my desk* and only separated by the thin walls without insulation or soundproofing. Every ten-to-twenty minutes, it seemed there was some activity outside with a helicopter. This went on for most of my tour. Of course, the papers we worked with and the ever prevalent dust inside would constantly fly around from the air current generated by the helicopter blades. We did not let the noise bother us inside as we went about our work, despite the fact that we wore no hearing protection.

However, I personally *liked* the sound of the helicopters. They were always a welcome sound and sight for me and meant that someone was probably going out somewhere on a mission, or coming back "home" from a battle, skirmish, or work assignment, or maybe even going back to the U.S. on the "Big Bird." No one went anywhere in the 101st without a helicopter. The pilots and machine gunners were everything that you saw in the movies… and more professional, on time, fearless, and with a sense of mission or urgency. **I never worried about a helicopter ride as I knew *I was always in great hands.***

This is a "Chinook," which was actually too large to land just behind my desk.
It was used for troop transport and "R and R" trips.
Courtesy of Randy Parmley.

Inside our building, there were floor fans strategically placed to keep the air moving because it could get very warm and oppressive, otherwise. Whenever Phu Bai would be hit with incoming rockets or mortar attacks, we would dive under the nearest desk.

When I returned from Vietnam, I was usually quick to comment that we only got hit *twice* a week…because I did not want to talk much about it and I did not want anyone to know how *every day of survival in an active war zone is a gift from God.*

The "incoming" was random, enough to keep us on guard, and could not be anticipated. Sometimes we got hit every day for two weeks and sometimes more than once a day. "Charlie" wanted us to know he was around somewhere out there, if only to keep us *on edge*.

With what the enemy knew about the terrain and our base layout, they could have overrun us any time, as happened in major South Vietnamese cities. We would have given a good fight but they had more man power to draw upon whenever they wanted to pull it together. Then you would have seen the full battle report on the 10:00 p.m. CBS, NBC, or ABC News back home.

They could have returned in a week to do it again and hidden away in their caves—the full extent of which we did not find out about until after the War. The *enemy* moved around and *chose* when to engage, when to retreat, when to wait, and when to disappear.

If anyone can get a good night's sleep in that environment, they are probably already dead.

CHAPTER 11

Day-by-Day

I had taken with me to Vietnam *The Power of Positive Thinking* by Norman Vincent Peale as I still had a few chapters to go after AIT. The religious studies and philosophy books by Reinhold Niebuhr, Martin Buber, Thomas Merton (*The Seven Storey Mountain*), Maurice Merleau-Ponty, (*Sense and Nonsense*), Martin Heidegger, Henri Bergson, and others all were, unfortunately, back home on a book shelf. Had I taken any of those books to Vietnam, only a few would have understood and I would just have been laughed at. They would have been comforting, though. They addressed the age-old questions of our existence and purpose in this life. As for John Paul Sartre and his *Being and Nothingness,* as George Orwell was to have said, I "gave him the boot," too, as I tried three times to read that book and could not get beyond page 60.

I had my abbreviated *Missalette* which I read for keeping balanced and focused on something more important than me, and I kept it in one of the oversized pockets of my Jungle Fatigues.

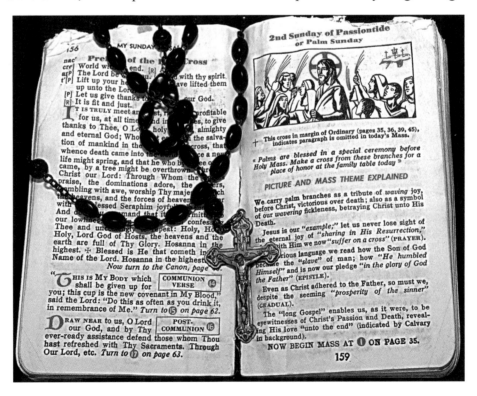

I started wearing the rosary beads after a few months. If I should lay dying, I wanted everyone to know that I was a Catholic and to get the Catholic chaplain. I know I carried a basic waterproof wallet with a card in it that identified me as a Catholic, but I needed all the help I could get when dealing with possibly minutes…or just seconds.

**This is what I wore, along with
the "red tag" allergy alert and later
with my rosary beads.**

Some of the guys wore the nylon or leather wrist-bands and neck-wear. That was not for me, but I did wear a very inexpensive water and moisture proof watch that I probably got from the "PX" (Post Exchange) for $5.00 in military exchange currency, as our "green backs" were illegal in Vietnam to minimize Black Market profiteering.

The Mess Hall food layout and schedule was easy to get used to. We had our daily and once a week anti-malaria pills to take with our breakfast. I did not know much about malaria except that I needed to take my pills which were laid out on the dining tables for us. I remembered my Uncle John Klimkos used to have his malaria relapses later on in life from the time he spent in the Pacific Theater during World War II, so I didn't need to be reminded to take my pills.

Being a creature of habit, I was used to cold cereal for breakfast at Penn State and also at home growing up. The problem at the camp was that *we just did not have milk most of the time* to go with the *Post Raisin Bran*, which was my favorite. I grew up reading the baseball and football cards on the back of the Post cereal products and I was hooked for life!

"The Mick."

We did have juice, though, and many mornings I poured apple juice on the *Raisin Bran*. It was not the same, so I ate it quickly without tasting what I was eating. Coffee and tea were available but I did not drink much coffee back then. Once in a while, I remember pancakes and hot breads, but I liked my cereal and had not learned about Belgian waffles or omelets…yet.

There were salt and pepper shakers on each table and the salt always had rice kernels in the bottles to keep the salt from clumping together from the humidity. The food was not memorable but it kept us alive. That is why all I remember is the cereal with apple juice poured on it. (Grapefruit juice was just too acidic to be poured on the *Raisin Bran*.)

The Vietnamese female workers kept the tables cleared and gave out "orders" to "sit here" or to "sit over there." We were told that we would get steak once a week and probably on Sundays for dinner but we did not get steak sometimes for months at a time. We had sliced water-buffalo meat with rice for a lot of the meals—except breakfast.

There was always dry cereal…and some fool who was willing to pour on apple juice! *Yes, I really did that.*

The rest of the meals were nondescript. If you did not make the scheduled meal times, you were out of luck until the next scheduled serving. You could not call out for a Chicago deep cut pizza or a Philly submarine sandwich with chopped New York steak, cheese, and mushrooms. But whatever they gave us had to be better than the soldiers going through the rice paddies looking to engage the enemy. There they only had the "C" rations.

As the first few weeks went by, I realized we had a regular newspaper coming in called *Stars and Stripes*. It was not like anyone said, "Hey, we get the daily over here!" but I saw some of the clerks reading it during lunch before we had to be back at work and I became inquisitive. I made it a point from then on to get my "daily paper," which some have considered a "sanitized" paper. This is because our government did not want to "telegraph" what we were doing to the enemy on the front page, and it wanted to keep the morale high by stifling negative news on casualties, battles, enemy activities, etc.

Back home, Walter Cronkite and others were showing on U.S. television sets *"the way it was"* in the War. In modern times with U.S. participation in some of the Middle East hot spots, soldiers can pull out their Smartphones and call their moms, Tweet their girlfriends, text their buddies back home, in between following the news on the Internet sites, and then go back to listening to Taylor Swift's or Zac Brown's latest hit which they have downloaded and saved. We did not know the full extent of what we were missing.

As the weeks turned into the first few months, I ventured up to the Post Exchange ("PX") only a few times for toothpaste, soap, pipe tobacco, and other incidentals. We did not have much free time after lunch and I had to get back to work always in a hurry. I remember the PX closing around 4:00 p.m. or 5:00 p.m. and we were still working then. Over time, I bought my own Sony radio and a few books to read. Most of the magazines seemed to be out of date. I have no way to know if we had the excised versions of *Time, Newsweek,* and *US News and World Report.*

I know we needed to keep morale going, and it was pretty easy to fall into a funk about why we were there and would we ever make it out alive? We did not need bad news from home on top of that.

No one as new as I was going to "go anywhere" for a while, but I do remember the Section Supervisor saying I had done a good job but it was not my turn yet to go to Da Nang for a day of rest and recreation (R&R) at an Army run facility next to the South China Sea. He said I would go the next opportunity he could send someone, which was sometime in April. I think I was rewarded with a trip to Da Nang three times during my tour, which turned out to be nothing like Ocean City, Maryland, or Miami Beach, Florida, but it still offered quiet and rest.

It was always fun for all of us to take the quick helicopter rides, but sometimes the stories would drift in of someone who worked in the 101st Admin Company getting killed in a helicopter incident. I still liked the freedom of the sky and the speed of flight and flew in the Huey Cobra or Chinook whenever the opportunity would present itself, which was eight or nine times in my tour. We were "Airmobile," and flying was sometimes the only fun thing to do over there. But that could get you killed, too, and it did not just happen in the movies.

The Personnel Clerk job was challenging enough and kept me busy and focused on doing something positive. Too much time to think can cause the mind to wander, especially in a war zone, but I will leave that story for the psychologists to write about.

A Huey Helicopter.

**Sculpture by Frederick Hart
near The Vietnam Memorial Wall,
Washington, DC.
Photograph by Carl Gernazio.**

CHAPTER 12

Amigos

Almost 90% of the soldiers I worked with in the Personnel Branch of the 101st Administrative Company had college degrees. Future studies since then have gone on to "prove" that the Vietnam Veterans were the most highly educated soldiers of all our wars to that point. That seems about right, as I could take the group of college graduates I worked with and succeed almost anywhere in business, education, or government.

With Personnel, I soon met my Team Leader, Larry Sindelar, who sat in front of my row of Personnel Clerks. Larry had his Bachelor's Degree from Loyola University and did not make a mistake as far as I could tell. I could not stand it, as he *had* to have a flaw, but I could not find one. He trained me well over the next seven-to-eight months to the point that I thought I was almost as good as he was in doing *my* job, but not quite. (I think he made one small inconsequential typing error the entire time I worked with him and we used to joke about it.)

Larry was an easygoing guy who probably spent the entire tour over there and had maybe half a can of beer in the entire year—and then maybe because he just wanted folks to think he was a regular guy. He ended up after the Service getting his Master's Degree from De Paul University and then went to work for a large software company from Atlanta, GA.

I served with a lot of really bright and ambitious guys, but Larry just stood out. He did not belong there but he made the best of it, and would have made a fine officer. Always working, never tired, he never used profanity or smoked, and was the model soldier I tried to be, but Larry was better. He always had the right answers, was as well organized as I was, and was the effective buffer with the Sergeant or Chief Warrant Officers who were the supervisors or managers. "Radar" from M*A*S*H had nothing on him!

Larry, who was my age, got to Vietnam six months before I did, and it is possible that he got a stronger dose of *Agent Orange* than I did, as he picked up his own cancer in his early 40's. He died in 2011 of the cancer complications. He left a widow, two sons, and a large company to manage.

We had seven or eight clerks on our team and there were three teams in Personnel. We had a different Sergeant in charge of each team plus a Team Leader. There were two Warrant Officers in charge of Personnel. As part of the 101st Administrative Company, we had additional units for Procurement, Budget, Finance, etc. I did not visit or wander around and usually stayed in my

chair at my desk or only talked or worked with others within my team. I had work to do and knew that if I was caught socializing or wasting time, I was going to be sent out to the field, as I was *expendable*. This really reinforced in me that I *needed* to be working all the time.

I look back with much pride at the group of men I served with in the Personnel Branch, our Team Leaders, and the Chief Warrant Officers in charge.

After receiving my MBA later, I served for nearly twenty-eight years in the federal government in Washington, DC for several agencies. Most of the last fifteen years were spent as a Human Resources Director, Personnel Officer, or as a Branch or Section Supervisor. But I never again came across such a hard working group of dedicated and knowledgeable workers as I experienced with the 101st Administrative Company.

They were the very best. **I served with the *best and the brightest* and we didn't have a slacker in the bunch.**

I tell the students in my classrooms now that it is not always what you know, as you have to remember the "social part" of work, too, which can help you to advance. With the Army, it didn't matter that much, as the Chief Warrant Officer in charge was one of the fairest and best managers I have ever worked for. I was not aware of politics while "CW-2 Evans" was our head. He did not like long meetings, kept on topic, and did not try to impress us with his personal stories, as he was all business. He smiled only rarely, but we were in a war zone and we had work to be done! Who cared if he did not smile, as it had nothing to do with our work. He was not auditioning for a TV game show.

I trusted all of these guys who were there when I arrived, and knew that my life depended upon them.

"Ike" had already kept me from playing soldier in the rice paddies, and he sat a few desks in front of me for most of my tour. I owed him.

CHAPTER 13

Early Days

It was a *war zone* so there was much value in keeping us busy in the Personnel Branch. It was good for mental and emotional health also, as we always had paperwork.

We worked seven days a week and our work day started at 7:30 a.m. We went to work in green Jungle Fatigues and sometimes took off the shirt top to just work in a green tee shirt. Our shirts, trousers, and underclothes were washed regularly and we had labels stapled on our shirts and trousers with our name. Sometimes the laundry people messed up and we got someone else's clothes. If it fit and I was in a hurry, I wore it, as most of us did not have the time or interest to run all around camp looking for just the right shirt. We were not picky and we did not have to worry about dressing up for girlfriends or wives. The regular soldiers did not have to be concerned anymore about spit-shining our boots, either, and although it was not "casual Friday clothes," like we used to do in the federal government later on, we were not about to experiment with anything that was not government issued. Everything was green that we wore, except the special jungle boots which were green and black.

We worked until lunch time and we were given 30 or 45 minutes for lunch. We had to be back by 1:00 p.m. and worked until 5:00 p.m. and then broke an hour for dinner and free time to read or toss a ball around. We then usually worked most nights of the week until 8:00 p.m. and went back to our sleeping quarters ("hootches") to play cards or read until 10:00 or 10:30 p.m. We were all pretty much up the next day at 6:30 a.m. to get ready for the new day. Some weeks, we only worked three-to-four nights after dinner at 5:00 p.m. If we had a chapel service to attend on Sunday, we were given 30-45 minutes and then were expected to come immediately back.

I remember that the Catholic priest would come by Camp Campbell only once a month for Sunday Mass as he was probably needed more out in the field. Sometimes, I was the only one at Mass, but usually a few others from the 101st Administrative Company would be there.

Often on Sunday, we did not work in the late evenings. Some Sundays, we only worked in the mornings, but most weeks, we were working 60-75 hours a week. This was real work time and not just "face time." I knew that I had chosen well to be a "Clerk" and none of us complained about the long hours.

It has been reported and generally agreed that *7-out-of-every-8* Service members in Vietnam served *"behind the lines"* or in *"support positions."* Of course, there were no behind the lines "safe havens" in Vietnam, as the entire country was in fact *"the war zone."* But not everyone was in the Infantry. Of the 2.7 million soldiers positioned within the borders of South Vietnam during the War, they either fought in combat (or) provided close support (and) were at least fairly regularly exposed to enemy attack. Sometimes, the heavy fighting moved around and wasn't very predictable. When I served at Phu Bai in 1971, most of the fighting was down in the south by Saigon. A few months after I left "I Corps," the fighting intensified around Phu Bai and Hue.

Day-to-day assignments usually began with the sometimes typed "Orders of the Day" from the Team Leader or Section Supervisor. Each clerk was assigned a 101st Airborne Division Unit for which he had to keep meticulous personnel records. I had the 3rd Battalion of the 506th Infantry Regiment and the 2nd Battalion of the 506th Regiment, in addition to special attachments. Men from both of these battalions were fighting in the *A Shau Valley* in *Vietnam* and along the "Ho Chi Minh Trail" in *Cambodia* and *Laos. I had to know this,* but I also knew that I could not be too detailed in making record entries. We were *not* supposed to be in *Laos* and *Cambodia* according to what we told the American people. Sometimes I was given the records for the 1st Battalion of the 506th Regiment to help out. I liked having more and more units to be responsible for as I liked to see how much I could handle and keep the paperwork filed as quickly as possible.

They were "my men" and I felt responsible for them. I wanted to take care of them the best way I could, which was through superior clerical service. If one of the soldiers died in my unit that I served, it also affected me.

As I look at these emblems today, as I am writing this book, I am very deeply moved by the legacy of the three (1ˢᵗ, 2ⁿᵈ, and 3ʳᵈ) Battalions of the 506ᵗʰ of the 101ˢᵗ.

**Insignias of the fighting units with the 506ᵗʰ.
Courtesy of Randy Parmley.**

Official paperwork or even slips of paper came in from the field or from another office on an individual's assignment, reassignment, transfer out, promotion, awards, temporary duty (TDY), death, battle campaigns, and citations. I had to make double notations for each action and file the paperwork in the proper personnel record. Records and index cards were to be alphabetized and arranged by organizational unit. If you got behind in your filing, lost a file, or the soldier was not identified in all the records as being in your unit, problems developed quickly as the unfiled paperwork just piled up.

Sometimes, records had to be updated by typewriter or special forms had to be filled out by typewriter. If there were multiple tissues or carbon copies involved, a borderline typist like me was going to have problems. At some point, I was given the approval to make notations in all capital letters in print for some of the paperwork. I still typed when I had to, but printing, not cursive, as no one could ever read my writing, became an acceptable alternative. Now the kids learn to type early in elementary school using *Mavis Beacon Teaches Typing Program* so that kids are learning the keyboard at a very early age.

For me, there was a lot of satisfaction in timely and accurate filing and recording which prevents future problems down the line. Growing up as a middle-schooler and teenager, I had my baseball-card, stamp, and coin collections and I had two separate paper routes delivering the *McKeesport Daily News*. I learned to be organized early.

As a requirement of our job, we had to lock up everything at night and *personally destroy every piece of paper,* as Vietnamese civilians were in the camp working and we could not trust any of them completely, as we did not know their alliances, personal history, political beliefs, etc. Leaving unsecured paperwork on any soldier or unit, if in the wrong hands, could be used to track our movements, plans, weapons, supplies, etc.

One morning a guard on the bunker line found our Vietnamese barber dead. He had been shot up by our side as he was coming with some friends through the concertina wire at night with wire cutters. He had cut my hair quite a few times, but I never needed a shave from him. He was probably quicker than I wanted to find out with a razor or knife, as he kept his skills and allegiance hidden.

We were warned that Communist sympathizers could be in the camp working in "our" laundry, Post Exchange (PX), barber shop, Enlisted Men's Club, in the Mess Hall, or used to dust and sweep our hootches. They also could have worked in the Recreation Center across the road. That was usually closed anyway, and the swimming pool water was *brown*, so I never went inside the "Recreation Center." I do not remember anyone *ever using it,* until maybe the last one or two months of my tour. It was "off limits" in my mind as too dangerous.

CHAPTER 14

Learning the Ropes...and the Perimeters

I remember being told early on not to "wander around" Camp Campbell unless I knew exactly where I was going. There was a major highway that cut through the camp that was frequented by Vietnamese natives on foot, bicycles, motorcycles, and maybe an odd truck. The enemy was around the camp so one would have to be pretty stupid to go out and wander around. The ancient imperial capital of South Vietnam, Hue, was just minutes away to the west (10-miles) but it was the target of the "Tet Offensive" in 1968 and was always ripe for an attack by the enemy. I had no interest in going to Hue. The U.S., which was the only place I longed to be, was 10,000 miles away and we all knew to stay in camp.

I remember the burning waste in wire receptacles all around camp where the Vietnamese women would collect and then burn the human waste to dispose of it. This seemed to be a daily routine and it did pollute the air with smoke, flames, and the smell of burning feces. I did not know what had created such an awful odor for many weeks and had no idea what was being burned until I asked one of my co-workers.

I sometimes said "Good morning" or "Hi" to the Vietnamese workers but I was not inclined to interrupt their routine or know too much about them. We were in their country and yet I did not feel any connection or kinship. They had a job and we had a job. The cultures were different, and the South Vietnamese were very poor. Several of the women chewed tobacco and some smoked a pipe or cigarettes—maybe something stronger, but I had no interest in finding out.

In addition to the main 101st Admin Company Building, we had the Mess Hall, latrines and shower area, and the hootches where we slept. The helicopter pad was outside the back of the Personnel Branch were I worked and the snack bar where they sold the yellow-brown ice cream was just a few steps away from the Administrative Building. There was a large maintenance building that had a basketball hoop hooked up outside where we sometimes shot baskets. I remember an indoor basketball hoop, but for some reason it seemed to be off limits to us. We did use it one time in a memorable game of "5-on-5" toward the end of my tour.

Mainly, I stuck to my routine of using just certain buildings and had no interest in getting lost, shot at, losing a limb to a land mine, or knifed by the enemy if I wandered off. We were told to travel in pairs if we went off the regular pathways and we were warned of the dangers. Twice, I remember riding in a green-brown camouflage jeep with another soldier as we had to supervise Vietnamese civilians on a cleanup assignment. I was not too fond of this assignment, as anytime you left the regular group of soldiers you could get killed.

Explosions, loud noises, or gunfire could be heard somewhere, it seemed, almost hourly during the day or night.

But we had all the comforts we needed right in our small work and sleep area. Who could need anything more?

Sometime toward the end of January, there was a new routine to learn with my job as a Personnel Clerk and living at Camp Campbell. I was not inclined by nature to take any risks unless I felt safe. I did not know beforehand any of my new peers or supervisors. I do not know where most of the guys from Basic Training and AIT ended up as I never saw any of them again. I did not want to stand out as a trouble-maker or know-it-all and I had to fit in quickly.

I watched what everyone else was doing for meal times, any free time, and what to avoid in camp. I was given a temporary sleeping section in the hootch and was told when a larger space opened up, I would be next in line to get it. There were six-to-eight of us in a hootch and we almost all worked in Personnel. There was an aisle down the middle of the sleeping areas and screens in the windows which allowed the air to circulate. There was a front and back screen door but I seemed to only have reason to use the front door as it faced the 101st Admin Company work building and washrooms/showers.

I had a large 5-foot high metal standup locker in my sleeping area for my M-16, ammo, maybe a wooden foot locker, poncho, and two small pictures of my family back home that I had taped up on the inside of the large metal locker door. I had my green duffel bag folded up in the wooden foot locker along with a light blue pair of trousers, brown belt, black Florsheim shoes, and a red shirt. The Army did not confiscate my civilian clothes—as they promised—and I was happy to have anything else from home with me.

I do not remember the soldiers in my unit having pinup pictures on the outside or inside of their lockers. During World War II, the guys kept pictures up of Betty Grable and Rita Hayworth. Maybe the Air Force guys across the way on the other side of camp had access to more magazines, but we lived in a pretty sterile environment in our hootches in the 101st Admin Company. Even Raquel Welch didn't get pinned up much in the 101st! However, any picture that was in the *Stars and Stripes* might end up on the wall back at the office, as one did for me....

I learned about using the green mosquito net immediately and kept my sleeping area tightly organized and minimal. Since it was never going to get very cold in the evenings, I made do with a regular green Army blanket and a nylon camouflage liner that was used like a bed cover. An extra blanket was kept in the metal locker but was seldom needed. I learned to sleep better with the rain, as it usually meant the enemy probably was not going to be as likely to visit the camp *en masse* at night.

Unlike police officers, guards, and firefighters in the U.S., we could not go back home to our wives, girlfriends, and families as we had to live and sleep in the war zone with no mental breaks.

I think this is what helps to wear one down quickly...we could not turn off the *High Alert* that we were in a *war*.

I do not remember doing daily exercises such as sit-ups, push-ups, or stretches. Maybe we should have all been doing an exercise routine each day just to combat stress. Some of the guys may have done that but we were all supposed to be in shape and were in fighting condition, most of us having just come out of Basic and AIT. Some of the soldiers at the higher ranks with us at the time were "lifers." They knew what they had to do to stay in peak physical condition to remain on active duty. I do not remember any runners or joggers, but I was not a runner at the time so maybe that is why I never noticed.

Roy and Gary at Phu Bai.

My buddy Gary catching a pass.

It was later in life that I learned the value of daily exercises and stretches, even adhering to a regular running schedule which I stuck to for many decades and I even ran when I visited Krakow, Poland later in the early 1990s. But when you are young, you think you will live forever and…always wear the same belt size! Now I know that daily exercise is very important!

Washing up in the morning and at night meant a short two-to-three minute walk to the sinks and showers in a separate facility. For eleven months we had cold water to take a shower. For a brief period, something happened and we had warm water during a two-week period of the summer. I think that came about because the sun warmed up the pipes and water storage tank and it did not rain to cool things off. We were never able to figure out that little mystery. We were grateful for the warm (not hot) water. And, at least, we could shower daily; the poor guys out in the field told us they were lucky to find a shower once a month.

CHAPTER 15

Battle Lines and Bunker Lines

The bunker system was set up around the perimeter of Camp Campbell. Bunkers were made of reinforced concrete and strategically placed to guard major areas of the camp. Usually, four soldiers could fit in a bunker. For the sleep shift, the flak jacket was taken off and could serve as a pillow. I did not learn that little trick right away.

One of the drawbacks to bunker guard is that you can have too much time to think. Then you may get depressed, anxious, nervous, maybe angry, and sad. The other drawback, though, is that you can get killed and "may not know what hit you," as the saying goes.

Every day I spent in Vietnam started off with a prayer.

I prayed throughout the day to survive. *You never know if today will be your last day.* It could be, but you do not know it when the day starts. You do prepare, though, for the worst and you make your peace with God. I did not personally know of any atheists in Vietnam but I did not get out of the Personnel Branch much to wander around to perform random surveys. There is a time for adventure and a time to stay put.

Bunker guard duty was rotated so that those who were trained Infantrymen had bunker guard duty every second or third night. I do not think I ever went more than four days without bunker guard. Duty started just before dinner, when we had to locate the bunker mates that were assigned via a typed-up schedule. Our group had to take a M-60 machine gun, ammunition, Claymore mines, and a battery with wires. Each soldier in the three or four-man bunker group took his own M-16, helmet with liner, ammo, and flak vest. It was likely to rain a lot of the time so ponchos and full Camouflage Fatigues were *de rigueur.* Every third or fourth bunker unit was assigned a "lookout tower" (Watchtower) to man for the night in place of a bunker. The lookout tower was 90-feet off the ground and contained special night-watch equipment and a telephone to alert the Sergeant in charge of "any suspicious activity on the other side of the wire." Once you found out who was on your team, you worked out a watch-and-sleep schedule so the workload was shared.

One of the first things to do on the bunker line was to set up the charges for the 50-gallon drums of *napalm* ("foo gas") and the M-18 Claymore mines. Both were directed outward toward the lines of concertina wire facing the direction that the enemy would come from. We usually had a supply of grenades in a box and possibly the LAWs, which could blow up a tank. I was acquainted with them, thanks to my AIT "dummy" testing. I liked best working

Setting up napalm charges on the Bunker Line.

bunker guard with Ike, who was dependable and my friend.

Sometimes, we took "Brutus" on the bunker line with us. Brutus was "a mountain of a dog" and probably part Mastiff and part German Shepherd. He took a liking to me and I liked him. We were all very fond of Brutus and encouraged him to "go with us" for the night of bunker guard duty. Often, he did not stay for the full watch, as he got side-tracked by meeting up with any female dog who showed any interest in him. Brutus helped detect and alert us to the smallest noises coming from the other side of the concertina wire protective shield that would at least slow down a full scale enemy assault, unless we were confronted with a full wave of "sappers" who could cut through wire about as quick as Jim Brown (Cleveland Browns and University of Syracuse football Hall of Famer) could pierce a defensive wall lined up against him.

In my *Rex* book, one of my Dedications is to Brutus:

"To Brutus, a mixed breed 'mountain of a dog,' who usually helped me guard the bunker line at night when it was my shift while serving in Phu Bai, South Vietnam in 1971, and the friend of many in the 101st Airborne Division."

Brutus at his "Bunker Guard" position.

We had to be on *High Alert* to the slightest sound or movement, as our lives, and the lives of our fellow soldiers, depended on it. We could not have an off night. Sometimes we imagined enemy movement or heard things. We had a protocol to follow if we knew or thought the sound source to be *human*. I am sure I said, *"Halt, who goes there?"* many times on my bunker guard. Mostly, it was another 101st Airborne Division soldier coming from another bunker to relay to us some important information such as anything that had been seen so far around the camp that would cause us to be on even higher alert.

We had two-way radios to communicate with the Head of the Guard for the evening and to work with the adjacent bunkers on any suspicious activity.

When it was my turn for the one or two-hour shift—which occurred once or twice an evening—I walked the bunker line on either side of my bunker, which was a distance of maybe 25–40 feet in each direction from the bunker. Infrequently, I sat on top of the bunker and looked out at the bales of wire. Before the sun went down was usually a good time to read mail from home while sitting on top of the bunker with the fully loaded M-16. I did not dare go to sleep while it was my turn to watch...but sleep deprivation was sometimes an issue for us.

In contrast, I often thought of how I enjoyed guard duty at U.S. Steel in Clairton, Pennsylvania in 1968, where they only gave me a "Billy Club." I used to walk for what seemed like a mile or two on summer nights when I worked in the Mill, moving around from the Blast Furnace, through the Benzene Plant, Rolling Mills, and on to the Tar Plant. I made sure things were locked up and that nothing appeared out of the ordinary. I had my two-way radio and a flashlight. I usually walked 2–4 hours on the night shift at Clairton Mill at a leisurely pace, and without fear.

Guard duty at Penn State my senior year had also been with a night stick and two-way radio. I used to walk the campus at night while on patrol, checking to make sure nothing looked unusual and that lab doors, especially, were secured. I already had some basics of guard duty, except, now, in Vietnam, it was with a loaded M-16, grenades on my belt, and this really was life or death.

With this kind of intense focus on our work over a sustained period of time, it is no wonder that some of us, including me, had great difficulty turning off the War mode upon re-entry into civilian life. As we all know now, some of the Veterans from any war never make the transition back successfully and can be triggered instantly into "life or death" panic mode.

Some bunker guard walks at Camp Campbell were under a high-powered light set well off the ground on a pole, but most of the time it was only star or moon light to work with. A lot of the time on bunker guard, I thought of home, and what I would do when I returned from Vietnam, and I would pray. Sometimes, I thought bunker guard was pretty easy as most nights were quiet in front of our bunker. Except for distant gunfire, war did not seem so bad—at first. After a while when you keep forcing yourself to pay attention to the slightest sound or movement—as your life depended on it and Brutus was only going to attack the enemy by going for the throat on your side of the concertina wire—you start getting "jumpy" and really start *worrying* if you are going to make it out of here alive.

If poor Brutus (I was expecting a lot from that dog) had to go into action that meant the enemy was within arm's reach and you better look for the bayonet attachment because they just broke through 50-feet or more of carefully laid out rows of large concertina wire strung together! With the inside dives, under the desk or chair, conditioning you during the day, the night time hyper-alertness to the slightest sneeze or flying bird begins to wear you down.

When our bunker guard duty was over around 6:30–7:00 a.m. the next morning, we were allowed an "extra" hour or two to eat and cleanup before reporting for work.

CHAPTER 16

Summer in the Camp

Toward April, a new guy showed up in our hootch and he brought with him his portable record player and only three albums: *The Greatest Hits of:* Tammy Wynette, The Four Seasons, and Johnny Cash. It seemed refreshing at first, but that's all the guy played. This went on almost daily, week after week for several months and on into summer. I liked all of these artists at one time but how many times can you stand to hear *Your Good Girl's Gonna Go Bad, Walk Like a Man,* and *The Orange Blossom Special?* By that time, the *Marriage of Figaro* by Mozart would have been welcome relief, and that is heavy opera!

I knew if I ever got out of this War I was going to have to write about this! Maybe I would not have gotten tired so quickly of Hank Ballard, Patsy Cline, Jim Reeves, and Smokey Robinson. Somehow, the new guy got quickly reassigned elsewhere and took his limited music collection with him. We were actually relieved.

With May and June, we started into the "thunderstorm" season and the higher humidity days. If it was going to rain, it could be heavy. The monsoon season seemed to run for a few months and ran through September and October, peaking in August. It did not rain every day over there…it just seemed like it. (My friend from undergraduate days at Penn State, meteorologist Dave Sage, checked his weather sources and believed we only had one monsoon season where I was stationed.) Dave was the first on our dorm floor back in 1970 to buy *Abbey Road* by the Beatles. When he cranked up the volume, I responded in turn with Janis Joplin and Big Brother and the Holding Company.

My "Rest and Recreation" (R&R) leave was still a few months off as I had to be "In- Country" seven to eight months before I could get a week's paid vacation to Bangkok, Thailand or Sydney,

Australia. I put in my bid for Sydney and enjoyed thinking about it for the next few months.

Phone calls home were more regular now, as I had figured out the times to call and how to do it. I think we were allowed to call home once every two weeks and the calls were limited to just a few minutes. I called my Mom regularly and if I did not call, she wrote that she thought something had happened to me. She did not want to hear my name mentioned by "Uncle" Walter Cronkite on the nightly CBS news! The calling system was prearranged with certain pick-up points. It was a mystery how the calls were connected up by involving ships in the Pacific, but it worked and I had nothing to worry about.

Some of the guys that were in the Personnel Branch when I arrived in January had already gone home, and new folks were always coming in. Around this time, one of the higher level non-commissioned officers who arrived after me at Phu Bai had begun to get more and more angry at little things, and was sometimes drinking too much.

We saw how the War was wearing him down—something which I started to be aware of more and more in *myself*, and in my buddies, too. Some of the guys were getting "too down," and had lost some of their energy and optimism.

Music was a salve for me. We could pick-up the Armed Forces Radio Vietnam (AFVN) at different points on the AM/FM dial.

I needed my music. It helped me get through the day easier.

There was a blend of R&B and other music, but I only listened to what I liked and smoked my pipe occasionally while I worked. I do not think anyone listened to classical music over there (except one fellow who liked opera) and I do not recall ever hearing it over the radio. The war zone was no place to bring my Beethoven, Tchaikovsky, Schubert, Brahms, and Ravel long-playing (LP) records, but it might have helped everyone's nerves on occasion.

I remember the afternoon DJ on the AFVN who played a lot of "Motown" during his 2–3 hour show. One time he played *Whatcha' See Is Whatcha' Get* by the Dramatics three times in a row and I have never heard that done again, ever. The DJ said it was "such a good song" that he was going to play it three times, and he did. The Temptations with *Just My Imagination* and gravely-voiced Rod Stewart's *Maggie May* got a lot of air play.

The Animals with *We Gotta' Get Out of This Place* was probably our favorite. We all sang along with Eric Burdon, and usually had a temporary work stoppage while the song played. I don't think anyone complained.

The song *Fortunate Son* by Creedence Clearwater Revival with its anti-war theme could make us laugh. I used to think I'd like to see old Mick Jagger over here and see how he coped with the War, if he thinks it is *bad* in England with his *I Can't Get No Satisfaction.*

Most of the money I made went back home to Mom and the family, as I had nothing to spend it on in Vietnam. Almost all of the recent draftees made the rank of Private First Class (PFC) as soon as we hit Vietnam. Specialist 4th Class would come for me six months later. With combat pay and overseas pay, it was better to send 90% of the money home. With my work group, none of us gambled and we all learned very quickly to live without the great luxuries of life back home. A radio, something to read, a pen, writing paper and envelopes, tobacco, a deck of regular or Pinochle cards, a beer here and there, and maybe a camera were all we needed to buy on our own. The Army was taking care of everything else for us.

However, it was not enough for some. One night while we were playing cards, the "non-com" came into our hootch, said a few inaudible words, and stuck his left hand into the middle of the open fan with blue plastic blades that had been turned on to keep the air circulating!

His blood was flying all over the hootch, settling on the walls, ceiling, and floor and we quickly sent guys out to get a Medic. The "non-com" had passed out in the aisle and the Medic soon arrived to care for him. He was carried out by three or four men and we did not see him again for another five months, when he stopped back to say "Hi" and showed us his healed-up hand. He had gone "stateside" to recuperate. Only he knows what he was thinking when his hand met the turning fan blades. When he came back months later, we had to move ahead, as we were survivors and could not dwell too much on negative *karma.*

Around this point, I had decided to pick-up the horseshoes that usually rested unused in the horseshoe pits that were about 20-feet from the side of our hootch. I waited nearly a half-year just looking at those horseshoes before I talked myself into trying something new. I threw by myself after lunch in the 5–8 minutes of free time we had and, after a few weeks, I could see improvement! Sometimes, others would join in and I could play against someone or in teams. I was not the best, but after a few months I was no longer a novice as when I first arrived.

Almost everyone I served with in Vietnam came from some other part of the U.S. and nowhere near my hometown. There were three to four guys from Pennsylvania but one learns quickly to get along with everyone and usually the talk after work or during a break was about wives, girls, sports, R&R, or music. These were more upbeat topics and took our mind away from the war zone. It seemed to me that about maybe one-third of the guys were already married with families back home, but I did not know the overall Vietnam statistics. Today, statistics show of the 58,000 killed, roughly 17,539 were married (30%).

One day I was in the back area of Personnel looking through the military records to see who would be processing through on the way to a temporary or permanent assignment elsewhere. I noticed a guy coming through from near my home town, recognized the name of the town, saw the test scores, and quickly recognized the last name. I will call him a distant friend and I made it a point to look for him over the next two to three days as he was in camp pending reassignment. I remembered that his Dad had also died when he was very young and his Mom had also received Social Security payments while he was in school. Unlike me, though, he did not go to college—yet he had scored extremely well on the Officer Candidate School (OCS) portion of the Armed Forces Entrance Examination. He had a Category I; my test score placed me in Category II.

I remembered that I did not try too hard on the test while in my senior year at Penn State as I did not want to get talked into going to OCS and going to Vietnam to be a Platoon Leader and getting knocked off first. I did not try to do my best on the test but still wanted to show the Army I had some brainpower without completely bombing out on the test as others had.

However, there was someone from near my home town, and I quickly found out that he had enlisted so that he would be able to pick his MOS (Military Occupation Specialty), which turned out to be something along the lines of a telecommunications expert. I met him and we shared a drink at the EM club. Quickly, he met up with someone who used hard drugs and they disappeared for two to three days. Not a word was spoken as to where they went. When he returned, nothing was ever said, and he went out to the field for his new assignment. I never had contact with him again.

But I did hear that he eventually received a General Discharge from the Army a few years later, got married a few times, had children, lost his driver's license, and died.

This Pennsylvania guy was a casualty of Vietnam…in more ways than one.

CHAPTER 17

Drugs and Booze

It seemed like it took us a long time after I arrived, but we finally started playing single deck Pinochle back in the hootch a few nights a week after our evening work. The game time might only be 20-30 minutes but it was something we could do together. Someone usually brought out the drinks to share. At some point, a small dinged-up, but serviceable, white refrigerator appeared in our possession and we packed it with *Cokes*, *Pepsis*, beer, and candy bars.

Someone found a football that Gary (University of Illinois) and I liked to toss around after lunch or after dinner. I think we only played two quick football games the entire tour and it was probably 2-on-1 because the guys did not seem to be into football. One time I ran into the concertina wire trying to catch a pass and I got my nose and chest hooked on the wire. I bled a little and three to four guys tried to help me off the wire. I think they cut off most of the wire and left a part hanging on me as they took me over by jeep to the Air Force side of the Camp.

There they had medical staff on duty to get the wire out, scrub out the cut area, and sew me up. I still have a bump on my nose today, but back then I was more embarrassed than anything else and went back to work the next day without further complications.

After I had been with the 101st for a few months, I found out about the "barbeques and beer parties" usually held on a Sunday afternoon. We did not have many parties that were attended by most of the workers in the Admin Company and we probably had one every two months or so. Steaks were usually promised but I would guess that half the time it did not materialize that way. Several garbage cans next to the Mess Hall were scrubbed down and loaded with ice, beer, and soft drinks.

As with that *"Agent Orange, no-need-to-worry"* business, I do not think we realized how *filthy* those steel 31-gallon garbage cans could become and how it was almost impossible to get them clean enough to "safely" hold ice and drinks.

I was drafted for "scrubbing assignment" once or twice and I think I decided to pass on the drinks later on. *Carling Black Label* seemed to be the only beer that we could get for the first six months of the tour and for some odd reason it was usually flat. That was not *Carling's* fault. We used to hear stories about how the beer sat outside in the sun for weeks or months on railroad cars in Vietnam before it arrived at its destination. I do not know how this was possible but I mention this to show the kinds of stories that were circulating all the time. If we heard it enough, it must be true, right?

I seem to remember that most of the guys ended up drinking the *Cokes* or *Pepsis*—and still out of the garbage can.

Rather than dumping all that *Agent Orange* spray on the land, we could have just given the NVA/VC the *beer* we had in those *chemical-laden* garbage cans!

The Army gave us a lot of the diphtheria/tetanus preventative shots in Basic and AIT. I think that is the only explanation for how we survived those "parties."

Around this time I started reading *The Greening of America* by Charles Reich, which one of my buddies in Personnel had recommended to me and who gave me his copy. It took many weeks to read, as I had Personnel Clerical work, bunker guard duty, letters to write home, Pinochle games, and the daily football tosses with Gary that were taking up all my time. President Nixon "still had not ended" the War, but he beat the Democratic Party candidate, George McGovern. Soon, however, "Watergate" finally caught up to him and he resigned just before I was ready to start work in Washington, DC in 1974 as a civilian in a federal agency in the block next to the White House.

Later on in my tour, I also read Joseph Heller's *Catch 22*, and *M.A.S.H.* by Dr. Richard Hornberger and W. C. Heinz. These books may have been from the small library or from the PX. I could certainly identify with the book setting and characters very easily. I think others were reading *Catcher in the Rye* by J. D. Salinger and *Farenheit 451* by Ray Bradbury, but I did not "meet" those books until many, many years later. It was my loss.

After straining from my desk for a few months over the helicopter noise and the constant hum of the fans to listen to the fellow's radio that was 10-feet in front of me, I bought my own portable multi-band Sony radio with built-in substantial speakers at the PX, and started listening to AFVN radio. The Muhammad Ali-Joe Frazier fight was about to take place on March 18 and I did not want to miss a single round although I was sure Ali would polish off Frazier in the second round. The fight went 15 rounds and Ali lost it. I could not believe it!

Regarding the drinking and drug usage, it was certainly present in Vietnam, but I can honestly say what I was exposed to was probably no better or no worse than what was going on at Penn State and most of the colleges and universities in the United States at the time.

Rather than give a fixed number of alcoholic drinks consumed, I will just refer to "drinking" or, as I call it, *"self-medication."* Once a college professor gave us the number of mixed drinks he consumed one afternoon while waiting for an airplane flight to attend a business meeting. He said he realized he had a problem after that and stopped "cold turkey." I probably think about that absurd number at least once a week. For some, one to two drinks is too many; others make a game of it and go for world class recognition. I do not want anyone reading this to try to match or beat a particular number. I remember most all of the numbers, but I do not want anyone to even think of "matching."

I had alcoholism in my family and so if you have a predisposition, you cannot always be doing what others are doing. But sometimes practice and theory are at a divergence.

There was a report in *USA Today* on August 5, 2013 citing *Princeton Review's* ranking of Penn State as number "9" in the "Top 10" listing of university and college "party schools" in the country. At least those Wisconsin Badgers at Madison were still ahead of Penn State in the ranking, but they have the "brewing capital of the world" (Milwaukee) staring at the Badgers from less than 90-minutes away. Despite being far removed from any big city with historic brewing or distilling enterprises, the tradition and reputation of being a party school has been carried on at Penn State through the decades. But Penn State also *taught* me a few things, too! My B.S. and MBA from Penn State certainly opened many doors for me.

I did not witness or hear about that much drug usage with the 101st Administrative Company at Phu Bai. Still, I remember a few incidents about drinking and drugs to show the fear, boredom, isolation from home life, repressed anger, anxiety, and depression. I will not use full last names in this book as, even if a Vet has passed away, family members are still alive and do not need to be embarrassed.

Some guys may have taken a beer or two on the bunker line but I do not recall that happening more than once or twice. It seems stupid, but if you have been going out there for month after month, some probably needed a sedative after a while. Toward the end of my tour, some guys took some marijuana on the bunker line duty, but I can honestly say this was also very isolated.

We had a strong drug enforcement policy in Vietnam. I do not know of any officers or Command Sergeants who tolerated drug use.

We knew if we smoked grass and were caught, we were in big trouble. Posters were always in full view about not taking a drug problem home with you, of the severe penalties, and of the likelihood of unannounced urine testing to detect drug use.

From articles in the *Veterans of Foreign Wars (VFW) Magazine* nearly four decades after the War, drug use among the troops varied by year, campaign, branch of service, and soldier's rank and "Duty Military Occupation Specialty" (DMOS). The soldiers I served with did not get involved with drugs except possibly the "later wave" of soldiers who came into the 101st Administrative Company as I was ready to return to the States.

Periodically, the odor of burning marijuana would appear in the hootch but never in the office. I never knew who was the supplier, did not care, and do not remember more than a few guys who relaxed this way. We knew of our drug testing policy. Sometimes a cigarette would be passed around and some continued to just pass it along and merely said, *"I'm good."* Others took a token puff. Only they know if they "inhaled." It did not matter that much. All of us wanted to fit in and blend together as a unit. We had to support each other and cover each other's back.

No one in the group that I worked with had the oversized ego to stand out from the crowd. Just like at Penn State, no one "ratted" on anyone and those who chose not to participate were not treated differently. I never saw any officers or non-commissioned officers involved. Some of the soldiers smoked, some drank, some prayed a lot, and some used a combination of whatever worked for them.

This social process occurred at the hootch level, in the Personnel Branch, and in the 101st Administrative Company as a whole. With ongoing transfers in and out, small and large groups had to continually evolve and adjust. Especially at the hootch level, we had to look out for each other more, and *protect ourselves,* as there was no supervisor or leader with us.

If someone had some personal issues, we had to be alert to danger and safety. Turning in a buddy was not an option and never happened with my involvement. Fighting and threats were different.

We probably had a few more "G.I. parties in Vietnam" where we cleaned out the germ- laden garbage cans again and threw in cold drinks and ice.

The tops of the pop-off cans would float in the crud from the garbage cans.

Once or twice, I remember one or two additional parties in someone's hootch where twenty-five to thirty guys would gather. I bought crackers and some generic *Spam* at the PX as my contribution and helped set up the party a few times. We would bring out red or blue "mood" lights, and during the party, guys would take their index finger and thumb on one hand and spread them about an inch apart to show they were "short"—which meant *they were going home at some point soon.*

Going home was always foremost on our minds.

We always had work to do so we did not really get to party too often. One incident I remember regarding booze and drugs took place when I had a toothache that had been bothering me for a few days. I received permission to be driven over by jeep to the Air Force Base medical station. The dentist who worked on me said he was going to use an "experimental procedure" because this was a war zone and the Army wasn't going to "dump a lot of money into my mouth." I thereafter called this the *"Vietnam Special"* after the dentist took care of my pain.

The tooth was never touched for almost forty years until my Vancouver, Washington dentist replaced the cap! What he found led him to believe that the mummified nerve had survived nearly forty years, when the intent was probably to permanently fix the tooth within a year—which would have been as soon as I returned to the mainland! (We requested my medical records on the dental procedure from 1971 at Phu Bai but the medical records the Army maintained on me lacked detailed specificity on that procedure.)

On the way back to the Army side of Camp Campbell, the driver and I made a few stops to see his friends from the Air Force. We visited a few living and sleeping areas and commented on the "Centerfold Collection" hanging on the walls from a popular adult magazine. They obviously had a bigger PX than we did . . . *with more reading offerings.*

In one of our stops, we entered a large kitchen area in the early afternoon that was unoccupied, except for many partially empty or empty bottles of hard liquor, wine, and grape juice, and the capper—*"pure grain" alcohol.* What was left of the mix was in the sink which stood about four inches deep. It was reddish-purple and had lemon or grapefruit slices floating on the surface. One survivor of the party reluctantly appeared and said everyone else had gotten sick and went to bed.

I was offered a sample in a white cup, took a small mouthful, and then spit it out in the cup! It obviously packed a wallop that was a concoction with about ten brands of liquor or wine. This was a new one for me as I had not even seen anything like it at Penn State. It was 2:30 p.m. in the afternoon and the driver took me back to the 101st Airborne Division side of the compound. Only those who have tried "pure grain" alcohol know what to expect, but I chose to pass on my lone opportunity as it was not something I needed to try.

CHAPTER 18

"Mail Call!"

_____

As with most in a war zone, I liked to get letters from home and especially packages from Mom with homemade poppy-seed cake, cookies, pretzels, and carefully wrapped homemade fudge or brownies. I always shared the food around, as others did for me. I had many aunts, uncles, and cousins I wrote to on a regular basis. One time my Uncle Todd Klimkos wrote back that I had sent him two different letters in one week and he wondered if I was OK? He had been in the Korean War as a Chaplain's Aide. I did not have a romantic relationship back home, but did write regularly to one lady friend who wrote back sometimes every day.

Even if you had to invent a girlfriend—not that anyone would ever do such a thing!—it had social utility with the guys.

Mail often came while we were already positioned on the bunker line, so I sometimes read the mail while pausing to look out in the distance at the rice paddies, the slow moving water buffalo, and the Vietnamese farmers still working.

When the mail was handed out, the messenger (or, the soldiers in front who used to pass back the mail) would comment on the handwriting, make a remark or two about the sender or recipient, and comment if any traces of *perfume* were still on the *envelope*—if from a female.

Mail Call was a big deal.

The following are two remnants of letters from my Mom....

"**I tried to send you some juice, but couldn't get it in this pkg.
-- here's what's in this pkg. Rat Poison, RAID for roaches,
toothpicks, thermometer, cake and cookies, Jello,
a little apricots and raisins (for) Jello, and some juice in small can,
so I'll send another pkg. with some Tang and different cookies in July.**"

"**Colleen and I went to see Mrs. Sedlak Thursday. They live by the river near where Honick
lived, do you remember? …went back the 15th of June to Chu Lai. …said he has Jungle
rash all over his legs and around his croach [sic]. (AUTHOR'S NOTE: This was a friend of my
brother Bernie's, who was a weight lifter.) I hope you don't get that. If you do get some
Boric powder and put on after a shower if you get a shower.
Well Jim everyone said to say hello. take care of yourself.
Be good. Bye now.
Love you, Mom, and all.**"

And one from my Godmother and Aunt Leona regarding my promotion from Private First Class (PFC) to "Specialist 4th Class" (E-4) mid-term through my tour.... (AUTHOR'S NOTE: Once you are "in" the Army, you are designated "E" whether you enlisted or were drafted.)

**"Congradulations (sic) on your promotion. I'm glad for you.
Hope you made out O.K. on your inspection."**

Both hold treasured memories, and deeply-felt gratitude for being loved.

**View from the Watchtower,
Phu Bai, South Vietnam**

All Along the Watchtower

"There must be some way out of here"
said the joker to the thief

"There's too much confusion,
I can't get no relief
Businessmen, they drink my wine,
plowmen dig my earth
None of them along the line
know what any of it is worth"

"No reason to get excited,"
the thief he kindly spoke
"There are many here among us
who feel that life is but a joke
But you and I, we've been through that,
and this is not our fate
So let us not talk falsely now,
the hour is getting late"

All along the watchtower,
princes kept the view
While all the women came and went,
barefoot servants, too

Outside in the distance
A wildcat did growl
Two riders were approaching,
the wind began to howl

Bob Dylan
Photograph by Baron Wolman

CHAPTER 19

On the Watchtower

July 1971

July 4th was our Independence Day back in the States.

In South Vietnam, we were on *High Alert,* as I seem to recall, as the enemy just might want to surprise us with its own "fireworks display." The Viet Cong/North Vietnamese Army (VC/NVA) was unpredictable and sometimes you could almost guess where they would hit next. Some of the Americans did celebrate with tracers. (Tracers are dummy rounds where burning powder is visible to the human eye, and parts of the sky light up with red and orange.) With a machine gun belt feeding through, a tracer is every 5th round, so you can tell where you are with your shot in relation to a target. Sometimes, tracers were used by leaders to show others in a group where to fire.

I continued with my regular assignment of bunker guard duty and really liked volunteering for the Watchtower as nothing much had been happening *up to that point* on guard duty. I liked to look out from the high view point 90-feet up to oversee the rice paddies, the farmers, and the water buffalo hard at work. Sun rises could be spectacular with the sun coming up over the South China Sea. I remember first hearing James Taylor's *Fire and Rain* one early morning in the Watchtower thinking it was written just for us serving in Vietnam. The lyrics and tone of *All Along the Watchtower* by Bob Dylan seemed to capture what the War meant to those of us who had Watchtower duty in Vietnam.

**A "gorgeous sunrise" view from the
Watchtower at Phu Bai.**

And then, just as easily as you can follow along and get lost in the hypnotic words and haunting melody of the song, there was one night before Midnight, when I was in the Watchtower alone, when suddenly, there were *hundreds of green (I thought blue-green, too) enemy tracers* that began to appear in front of me coming from about 400-feet away. They came at me from two distinct starting points at least 50-feet apart! It was like a dream sequence and I froze. Everything seemed to be in "s-l-o-w" motion.

They followed a fairly clean and predictable trajectory and whizzed by me as I was in the Watchtower. I knew I was in trouble if anything hit the tower, as I was high above ground and the fall from the tower would kill me…*if* a bullet or two couldn't. I thought of firing at the source of the tracers but realized that would only give away my position even more—if they hadn't already scoped in on me yet with their machine guns. There appeared to be two guns firing my way!

Behind me a few hundred yards away was the Air Force Base—part of our camp compound. It is possible the target was the Air Force Base and I was just "in the way," based on the direction of fire.

I thought the enemy was after me and this was how it was all going to "end."

I called the Sergeant of the Guard and screamed that I thought it best if I got *out* of that Tower right away, as I was not able to shoot without getting shot in the process from superior enemy resources! There was just too much fire power coming my way and the tracers were speeding by—above and alongside of the Tower. The Sergeant gave me an "Order" to "stay put" and "lie low" and to "keep my line of fire limited to incoming." He confirmed that he also saw the tracers coming in.

The incoming stopped after about fifteen minutes. I stayed in the Watchtower the rest of the night as I was "ordered," and realized that I had come close to meeting my final destiny. One of our silver-and-blue dress pins from the 101st read, "Rendezvous With Destiny." I could have gone out of the Watchtower and chickened out, by running away, but I *held my watch,* although I minimized my field of fire by laying down. *I met the test.*

In the morning, I walked down the wooden steps still shaking, dusted myself off from the garbage and debris I tried to hide under while being put to the test to see if I could "take it" being shot at. Then I went in for my breakfast and then on to work.

Now that I type this up, I do not know why another soldier was not with me in that Watchtower at the time. Maybe my partner returned later, but that was not the issue. I do know that the Sergeant climbed up the ladder at 2:30 a.m. (I first thought it was the VC coming up for me!) to "see" that I was alright and to commend me for "staying in the Tower" so I could "do my job," which was serve as a lookout post.

For probably the next thirty-five years, I dreamt periodically about being shot, and would wake up in a sweat, trembling.

After I finally realized it was the Watchtower incident, which only lasted fifteen minutes tops, I came face-to-face with the fact that I had survived. Then I was ready to move forward, certain that the incident no longer had a grip on my psyche. Somehow I had been blocked for all that time.

COMMENTARY: As I was working on this book, I saw Jimi Hendrix perform on "PBS" playing *All Along the Watchtower*…and I watched the hairs on my left arm jump out straight! I didn't need to look at my right arm. Hendrix's interpretation of the song was stunning.

I had once heard that Jimi wore the "Screaming Eagle" patch of the 101st Airborne Division on a jacket, and, as I heard him singing, I remembered my patch and how proud I felt wearing it.

The meaningfulness of the music Hendrix sang – and his guitar riff – transported me back to the isolation, the sense of futility, the fear of death…just as that night in the Watchtower.

**"Rendezvous With
Destiny" Pin.**

**The Sydney, Australia Opera House,
almost finished, 1971.**

CHAPTER 20

"R & R"

Sydney, Australia…Here I Come!

Finally, it was my turn for "Rest and Recreation" (R&R) in Australia, so I and four others were taken by helicopter to a small airport in Vietnam and then we flew on to Sydney. Everything was prearranged and that is the great thing about the Army. I do not even recollect the name of the airport, but it was probably Da Nang.

My first night in Sydney I remember the dance hall we visited which stayed open until 3:00 a.m. or 4:00 a.m. I found one lady from nearby Sydney whom I danced with most of the evening on my first night out of the War. Stevie Wonder's *Up Tight (Everything's Alright)* was played many times through the loudspeaker system. It seemed like it was played every third song, but I did not mind.

There were dancers in "cages" on stage, and in the balcony. A large multi-colored ball, which was suspended from the ceiling, was constantly turning in the middle of the dance area with strobe lights adding to the effect. It seemed like something right out of *Hullabaloo*, which was a popular music-themed TV program in the late '60s.

I only had a week in Sydney so I did not want to waste it sleeping, although I never thought I would live long enough to see a bed without a mosquito net and Army green.

I remember the bright colors of the hotel room and the city. I also remember how quiet it was, and peaceful. We had to walk a few blocks from our hotel down a brick street to get to the nightclub and restaurant part of the city. I checked out the water flow in the bathtub in my hotel room to see if the water really emptied, going opposite of the way it drained out "north of the Equator." I could not tell conclusively.

I had not seen a flushing toilet for *a long time,* but I did not forget how they worked!

I bought some new pipe tobacco (*Mac Baren's Plum Cake*), went to the zoo, and saw the kangaroos and Koala bears, went on a cruise, walked part way across the bridge leading to the construction of the new Sydney Opera House, and listened to music. A song by Lee Michaels, *Do You Know What I Mean?* was out and getting a lot of airplay in Australia and the U.S at the time. I remember waking early one morning for a walk toward the bridge leading to the almost completed new opera house. There were two drunks passed out around 7:00 a.m. with almost-empty bottles of green mouthwash on the ground.

My friend Ron, who joined me for part of the trip, said that when money is tight, the alcoholics drink mouthwash because of the alcohol content. It probably tasted better than that "purple drink" back at the Phu Bai Air Force Base!

Ahhhhhhhhh....

Sydney was a welcome relief from the day-to-day *High Alert* mode we had just left. Our small group went to the beach twice.

I think I went out every night to meet people and to dance with the Australian girls. There was one place called "The Texas Tavern" that we visited several times for "Happy Hour" in the afternoon. During this time, all *Cokes*, *Pepsis*, or alcoholic drinks were free for one hour. The only problem was that everyone was lined up at the bar and only a few ever got served during that hour.

My friends and I surveyed the situation and I decided that if I tipped the bartender with a very visible quarter, I would get my drink. It worked and I used this technique a few times. I had broken the "norm," but soon others caught on, imitated my behavior, and I did not stand out anymore. I flashed a dollar bill toward the end of "Happy Hour" and that worked.

I learned a few lessons there. **If you do not stand out somehow in a crowd or group, you may not get recognized. I saw this work in the "Dog Show World," too, many decades later.**

Unfortunately, this brief respite came to an end very quickly and I boarded the plane back to the War. I can see why some soldiers might go "Absent Without Leave" (AWOL), as Monty Cliff did in *From Here to Eternity,* but that was not an option for me.

I still have my Australian paper money and coins as reminders of my welcome break in the War.

I also have a postcard sent to my Mom.

"Sydney   Tuesday, 12 Oct 71

Dear Mom and all,

    We arrived in Sydney via Pan American at 9:00 a.m. yesterday. The temp is in the upper 70's and the scenery is beautiful. We expect to take in some swimming before our 7 days are up. Last night we did some dancing at one of the local discos. This afternoon I plan on taking some pics. I hear the Pirates lost first game of Series – nothing more…. I'll write again when I get back to Phu Bai.

                                    – Jim"

Sydney was a welcome relief from the constant stress and uncertainty of the War. Unfortunately, my vacation ended after one week. This picture was taken outside the hotel where I stayed, but I couldn't forget that I had to return to Phu Bai.

As I gaze at this photo below, I realize that I had *grown up* a lot from the *young college kid* who had arrived in Vietnam nearly a year before.

CHAPTER 21

Autumn Comes to Phu Bai

I started off the month of September by drinking too much cheap champagne that I had picked up at the PX to celebrate turning "23" on September 5th. I had a headache for three days and realized I could not afford any more days like that if I wanted to finish out my tour in one piece and walk down the exit ramp off the "Big Bird."

Back in the War, a few new guys had come in while I was off on R&R. Of the soldiers who joined us late in my tour most seemed to have become a "Personnel Clerk" in AIT and were not college graduates. That meant they were a little "greener" (younger) and had some rough spots not healed by four more years of adulthood. One fellow in particular from The Great Lakes area liked to tell us his tall tales, even if we did not want to hear them, as he thought he could impress us more with his "macho" stories. I did not like him much at first, as he had not "been around enough" to be considered a subject-matter expert on anything, and had a lot of growing-up to do. He liked to smoke anything he could get his hands on and was fond of his alcohol. I do not know how he figured out where to get his marijuana but he was very soon a daily practitioner.

Of all the sayings and pearls of wisdom that he dispensed, one stood out and did make sense. He said: *"Almost every male grows up thinking that he is the best, the strongest, the fastest, but, eventually there is always someone he meets or competes against that is better than he is."* That made sense to me and, from that point on, I saw a reason to be his friend!

You never know from whom you can learn something valuable.

By extension, too, some of us are brought up thinking, and having reinforced, that we are the smartest. Over time, you mature and find that there are folks that can do things better than you, if not just as well. It may just mean you have to work harder and have some things to concentrate on getting better at. Even after this guy nearly burned down our hootch later on, he was just a regular guy trying to fit in. We were *all* trying to fit in. For him, he thought he needed to show us how *tough* he was. He was "full of himself" at first but we came to appreciate him, and protected him with his…uh…"little habit." He always wore a white tee shirt; he should have been wearing Army green like the rest of us.

Another new guy that just showed up in our hootch one day around this time was from New York City. He was fast-talking and moved quickly. He also, as it turned out, had equally quick *fingers*…we could not catch whomever was taking the cold drinks out of our small fridge in the hootch. He was, though, suspect number one. I got tired of putting a single warm can of *Coca Cola* in the fridge to chill it, only to see it disappear before I could retrieve it to drink. The "original" *Coke* was pretty good and I was going to fight for it. This went on for a few weeks and I talked to the guys about the disappearing drinks, but no one knew anything. I believed that everyone should pay their own way—if they are able to. I then put a note on one of the cans with a rubber band in my best handwriting which read:

> **"Whomever takes this can of *Coke* better have a full life-insurance policy in place, with a designated beneficiary."**

The kid from New York appeared, opened the fridge, grabbed my can, and started reading my note so loudly he could be heard by almost everyone in the hootch.

I moved a few feet in front of him and told him, "That's my *Coke* and you have been stealing my *Coke*s for weeks!"

He said, "Well, I don't appreciate the death threat and let's see what we can do about it."

Words were quickly exchanged, and he soon made a flying leap to hit me, as I was about 15-pounds heavier and maybe a few inches taller. He missed, and I went right into him with my fist—which he effectively blocked. That was all we were able to manage before three guys were on him holding him back, and two guys were at my side. The rest of the hootch had heard the whole story.

He ran off to immediately whine to the CW2, and I was summoned within minutes "on the carpet" for my side of the story.

The CW2 said to me, "I want you to know that I view this matter seriously. If you create any more problems, you'll be headed straight out to the field. You were, after all, fully trained in AIT to be an Infantryman."

As for the guy from New York, all he was probably good at from his training was being a Personnel Clerk and there was really nowhere else to put him.

The CW2 told me, "Look, I have to keep this other guy, but I do not have to put up with you if you act up again."

I saluted the officer. "You won't have any further problems from me, Sir," I assured him.

And he did *not*, as I learned he considered that I was the one who had stepped over the line. To help the situation, however, "New York" swapped hootches with another soldier and this was better for all of us. We had no more problems, although sometimes I heard "New York" muttering at me under his breath. I did not bite at his provocations and ignored him. We never had bunker guard duty together and that was fine. He was just a punk, but he was street-smart and knew when he had more cards to play than I had.

Sometimes, you just have to walk away.

Around this time, "Bear," another basketball-playing buddy of mine from Texas, also got into trouble. I forget his name, but he had his college degree already and was a good, dependable worker. Although the Army has height and weight standards, this fellow was at least 6-feet, 4-or-5 inches tall. If he wanted a rebound, it was his. For some infraction— which we never found out about—he was shipped out immediately to the field to serve as an Infantryman with the 101st.

After we had asked about his whereabouts for a few days, we were told he was sent out to the field. I was able to see him after he was gone for about a month. He came in along with his small unit and visited a few of us.

He said he had not had a shower or bath the entire month, had lost a lot of weight from stress and dysentery, and told us it was "crazy" out there.

He warned me to do whatever I am told and not to talk back or fight back. He said, "You do not want to come out here where most of the action is."

I told him, "I already learned my lesson, and came pretty close to screwing it up."

I never saw him again and do not even know if he made it back alive. He was a good man and athlete.

CHAPTER 22

"The Boxer"

Picking My Fights

By the time Fall was ending, I began to realize that most of my problems seemed to come with this "last wave of men" who were fresh out of AIT and trained as Personnel Clerks. I was also aware that I was getting *edgier* and *less tolerant* of nonsense... not a good "prescription" for staying alive in a war zone.

Vietnam does toughen you up rather quickly, or you collapse mentally. Each of us went through personal character tests with exposure to a unique set of problems, issues, or jobs to contend with.

The main objectives are to survive and... to do your job.

If you train yourself to be optimistic and not to dwell so much on what is going on around you, you can make it out of there with luck and the grace of God. You need both. Learning a new set of skills and "self-discovery" are a bonus but will only help you get through.

I think that the core values that you take into a war are tested.

Weaknesses can be exposed and strengths built upon.

I remember wondering *"how the War was going,"* because we were right in the middle of it. I was not paid to *think* about such things, but I had an inquisitive mind.

You cannot walk up to a Full Bird Colonel or General and ask, "How's it going?" or "What is our next plan of attack or troop movement?"

Down through the history of warfare, generals have kept their own secrets and counsel for fear of getting information in the enemy's hands. Troops are told things when and only if they need to know, like when it is time to be on the march, or pack up and move to another location. But we were not supposed to make problems or appear to *be* a problem, so I went back to my reading, if I had any free time, and tried to forget how the overall War was going.

Around this time, "The Boxer," a guy from Florida, came to camp and started making his own rules as he went along. Whether he boxed or not, the fellow *was* a physically imposing specimen, was smart, and he had a quick temper, too. I do not know if he did too much work in the 101st but our main goal was to stay out of his way. He looked like if he got into an argument he would just as soon shoot any of us without a second thought.

Within a few weeks of his arrival, one of the Sergeants on the bunker line was shot and killed by someone *on our side.* That is about all we were told that we were sure of. Most of us in the camp who were not officers thought "The Boxer" had killed the Sergeant. The story circulating was that the guy was doing drugs when the Sergeant approached him on the bunker line. There was an argument and the Sergeant was shot. We waited for *justice*, but no charges were ever filed.

What *did* result from this incident was that *we* had to turn in all our weapons and ammunition to a central point!

Whenever we had guard duty, we had to "sign out" for the weapons and return them in the morning. If we had an "orange" or "red" alert—and we had those throughout the year—we had to first *line up to sign out for our weapons,* while hoping the enemy...would give us time...to let us *get* our guns!

This did not make any sense to me. I had gotten used to having the M-16 around and resting under my bed or two-feet away from me in my storage (gun) cabinet, and *now* we were *stripped* of our weapons! We accepted our new circumstances, but not without some grumbling.

"The Boxer," on the other hand, continued on with his ways. For several weeks, he actually had a Vietnamese woman living in the hootch with him who took care of him. A few mornings around 6:00 a.m., I would see someone dressed in blue-and-white or pink-and-white clothes and I came to learn quickly it was "The Boxer's" Vietnamese girlfriend. Now, he did not come to work until 11:30 a.m. each morning and then he went to lunch. After lunch, he went back to his hootch and did his drugs, only to reappear at work in the late afternoon. This went on for a long time, but I was not reporting him and it appears no one else did either. He wasn't even on my team.

One night I had the misfortune of being assigned bunker guard duty with him and one other guy.

I asked him, "What shift do you want?"

He responded, "I do not *do* bunker guard, it's not *my* thing."

I tried reasoning with him, and then said, "It's not fair that two guys have to do all the work to keep us all safe. We are *all* in the same Army and the same War."

I held my ground without losing my cool as I was not backing down, boxer or no boxer. To my surprise, instead of the two-hour shift that was required of each of us, which would have been fair, he actually put in *an hour* of bunker guard duty with me! I thought I had done pretty well and was pleased with myself. I did not get shot at, either, like the Sergeant ended up. "The Boxer" was tough to deal with, but I was not going to make him *my* problem.

You pick your battles, settle for your best deal, and you have to know when you are outmatched. You have to survive and be able to walk away.

Around this time, I started worrying about where my friend "Ike" was disappearing for large blocks of time when he should have been at work on our team. We were "covering" for him, but we could not keep this up forever. He would be gone for *hours* at a time, but not say anything about where he had gone.

One day with *many* more weeks to go in our tour, I found him sitting in the latrine *crying*. He said he went there "a lot" because the War had *worn him down*.

I talked to him and I told him that his secret was safe with me. I owed him.

Soon afterward, another kind of War-maladjustment took place. A married fellow came into our Personnel Branch and it was obvious from the beginning that he missed his wife and family back home. He would just lay on his bed some afternoons without any clothing and remain motionless under the mosquito net. It is just what the War *does to you.* . . .

Some guys get paralyzed with the fear or need time to zone out. After we had our M-16's taken away from us, I was more *afraid* than ever before. It was going to take us 30-minutes to line up to sign up to get our weapons and by *that time* the enemy could have shot us all! At least for me, things had really begun to *deteriorate* with "The Boxer's" arrival. I did not feel that safe anymore.

I was becoming more and more angry at the circumstances thrust upon us.

One afternoon as I was going out for bunker guard duty I found a small, clear-plastic, 1-inch vial container and could not figure out what its purpose was. I remember smelling the white contents and getting very sick to my stomach soon afterwards. I was almost doubled over in pain for three days and thought I was just going to die there. I was worried about the drug testing and how no one would "believe" I just "happened" to stumble upon a vial of something. Miraculously, my stomach pain cleared up and I do not think I could even eat for three days. I told one or two close buddies what happened and that I did not want the supervisors to find out. I was stupid to have tried to figure out the vial by smell.

By that time we had a new Camp Commander who was either a Lt. Colonel or a Full Bird Colonel (with a Silver Eagle Insignia). He was a very good manager and was well liked by all of us—despite the early formations on Sunday morning, which he reinstated, as we had not been required to do so for a long time.

I remember one Sunday morning he told us that "Colorado" had won their football game the day before and he was proclaiming them "Number 1" in the country. Since Penn State also had a very good team that year, I was not pleased that the polls had already closed with Colorado declared the "national champs" by the Colonel, with many weeks to go in the season.

He had with him as his Special Assistant a kid I will call "Sam." He was a "know-it-all," but he sure could play basketball and was the best over there. He knew it, too! I am not sure of his exact job description but he claimed to have a Bronze Star for something he did for the

Colonel. We did not want our medals that way—if he really did get a Bronze Star. To be honest, most of us did not like him. He seemed to be exempt from guard duty, and I think was the source of many unfounded rumors in the camp, which he started just to get us going.

I am *still* upset with the rumor he started that, "Brutus and all the other dogs were rounded up, destroyed, and then hauled off." He claimed to have "seen Brutus in the cage." This guy was of no use to us and was hurting morale. Sam also told us that one of our cooks had been shot down and killed as he was returning to the States from his tour.

It takes all kinds to make an Army. You get soldiers from different backgrounds, ways of doing things, ways of looking at life.

We left Sam alone and let him do his own thing, which was "*self*-promotion."

CHAPTER 23

"World Series"

Running Toward "Home"

It was "World Series" time back home, and the rains were starting up again at Phu Bai! The Pittsburgh Pirates and Baltimore Orioles were tied at three wins apiece going into the 7th game played on Sunday, October 18th. Although the game was on after Midnight, I listened to most of the game on my portable radio. I clearly remember hearing on the broadcast that my favorite player, Roberto Clemente, hit a home run in the 4th inning that stood up as the *only run* by either team for several innings, with the Pirates going on to win the World Series. It was about 2:30 a.m. in Phu Bai when Clemente hit his home run, which was the second of the Series for him.

It was about *four decades later* when I heard Pirates catcher, Manny Sanguillen, explain in a televised interview how Clemente, a right-handed hitter who hit to *right field* predominantly, had trouble with the left-handed curve-baller pitcher (Mike Cueller) jamming him on the wrists in that 7th game. Sanguillen said that Clemente squared around, adjusted his stance just for Cueller, and then sent one curve ball over the wall in *left-center field* for a home run! *You have to go with the pitch.* Forty years later, I finally saw a video about that same home run that Clemente hit in that 7th game…and, sure enough, the ball did not go to right-field like most of his *3,000* hits.

The odd thing was that there was no one I saw around the camp in Phu Bai over the next few days after the game, who was from Pittsburgh, so I had to keep my thoughts (and cheers) to myself about the Pirates winning the 1971 World Series. That was sad. *Sometimes you need to share great news.* After Clemente's home run in the 7th game, I thought of the baseball I had caught on a few bounces into the stands in the late 1960s after Clemente hit the right-field foul pole at Forbes Field for a home run. I also thought of the time I was walking behind home plate with Clemente at bat in another game at Forbes Field and I saw Clemente smash a line drive that barely eluded the outstretched glove of the second baseman. The ball continued to rise and barely cleared the wall, but it was a line drive home run.

I often think of the great arm, the catches, and how he carried himself on and off the field. He was also a great humanitarian. He died in January 1973, at age 37, while delivering relief supplies to Nicaragua refugees.

In another sport, toward the end of October, I remember the basketball players in camp got together to plan a game of 5-on-5 about two weeks away. We let the supervisors know of our plans so they would be "On Board" for this evening game, as we could not just all disappear at once. It was to be under the lights of a little used gym that we had found. The teams were assigned and I was on the team with playmaking and shooting guards, while the other team had the tall rebounders.

About ten days before the game, our star guard who was from the Pittsburgh area, was bitten by a moon-rat while playing Pinochle in our hootch. (This type of rat is generic to southeastern Asia, and has a distinctive pungent odor. It ranges in color from all white to mixed white-gray, white, and black, which is where the designation of "moon" comes from. It is huge, about 13-16 inches long, PLUS tail, weighing 2-1/2 pounds!)

**This is NOT an exaggeration!
These rats were HUGE and vicious.
Drawing by Ms. Leny Wendel,
artist and Samoyed owner from
White Bear Lake, MN.**

The rat had appeared from behind the wooden panel and bit him on the arm, and disappeared! At first, we thought he was joking. We got him over to the Air Force Base medical area and they started him on a series of shots in his backside or abdomen—I forget where.

The day of the game came and at the last minute—with still more shots to come for the moon-rat bite and still feeling weak—our guard from Pittsburgh joined us midway through the game, which *quickly turned our way* with his shooting and ball handling skills. The other side had gotten over-confident and began drinking beer early in the game, as they smelled an easy victory. As center, I got the rebounds, and the guards made the baskets, and we won using our heads to play a team game.

The guy from Pittsburgh went back to the hospital, finished his series of shots, and made a full recovery. We never got to play a game again with 5-on-5, but that one stands out of all the basketball games I have ever played in!

CHAPTER 24

Keeping Up

In November, someone showed up with a beat-up portable TV set, with aluminum foil wrapped around the antenna. I remember watching Bobby Majors returning a punt for a touchdown in a Tennessee football game and did not pay any more attention. We had read about *All In the Family* being a popular TV program back home in the early part of 1971 when it made its debut. I had no idea what the show was about and could not understand the fuss made in the U.S.

After a few months in Vietnam, you realize that you are getting behind the times and events are happening quickly back home that you will have to catch up on—*if you are lucky enough to get out'a here alive.* All your friends, family, and relatives are safely back home with their newspapers, televisions, stereos, 8-track tape-players, radios—keeping up with the advances in science, culture, sports, literature, business, and life.

Of course, we were *"making history"* over in Vietnam, but we missed our own culture and ways of doing things.

I wondered about previous civilizations and if they worried about "keeping up" with things back home in wars in distant lands as much as we did.

I did miss home and what I was familiar with and had been brought up around. Walks on the bunker line were not the same as the walks through the wooded area behind my home in Pangburn Hollow. I could just go up there for hours it seemed, and walk among the maples, oaks, and other hardwoods. At Phu Bai, there was no such option.

Back at the "office," change in personnel continued to occur. It seemed like more rapid turnover was occurring, but possibly it was just because everyone had been there for a while before I arrived with the 101st. So, before I could make friends with everyone, they were gone and back in the U.S. One of the new guys to our hootch and the Personnel Branch was a fellow from North

Carolina, who brought to Vietnam a tape of the "1969 Woodstock Concert" and a Neil Young tape. For the next month or so, we heard the entire lineup of performers on his tape deck, and that ran from Paul Butterfield, Santana, Janis Joplin, Richie Havens, Country Joe and the Fish, and on to Canned Heat, and Crosby, Stills, Nash, and Young. We were grateful there was no more push to listen to those other three artists from a few months ago! Still, Woodstock was getting "old," too, after many weeks. If we had been fed lobster every night for dinner, we would have gotten tired of that, too. It is one of life's ironies.

One thing for sure, though, *home* seemed very far away.

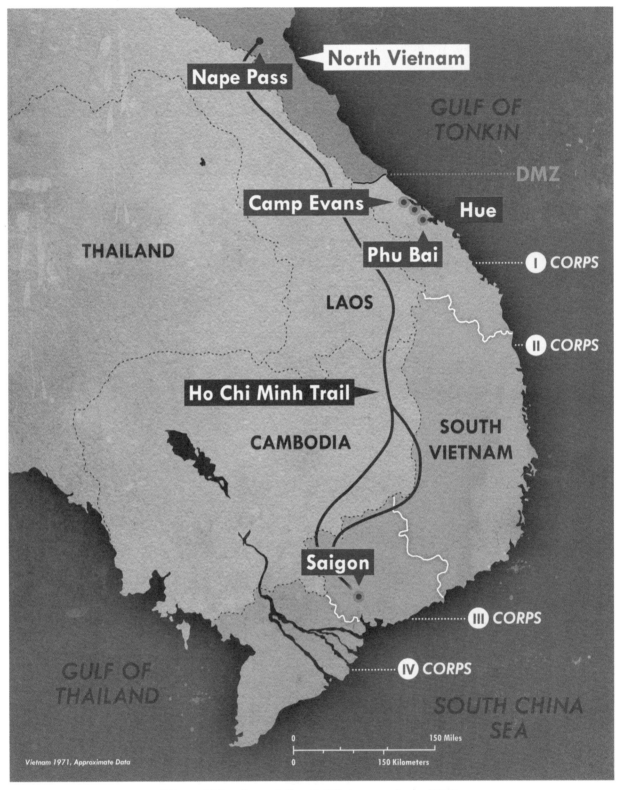

Map of North and South Vietnam, circa 1971,
by Brad Johnson.
In Vietnam we had four distinct Corps, and we all kept in communication with each other.

Camp Evans. Courtesy of Randy Parmley.

CHAPTER 25

Thanksgiving at
Camp Evans, Near "DMZ"

Thinking of home, more and more, it was also beginning to s*eem to me* that we had been *returning* more soldiers *back* to the States—at a much *quicker pace* and on a *larger scale*—processing-out unit after unit through the 101st Airborne Division at Camp Campbell. A request went out for "volunteers" to be a part of a new "temporary" location for processing-through this *increasing number* of soldiers "going home."

Because the soldiers were coming from the field north of us, the Colonel said it "made sense" for us to take this "out-processing unit" up north to Camp Evans, which was about as close to the Demilitarized Zone (DMZ) as a U.S. soldier would want to be! The Colonel asked for volunteers, and I remember thinking that I was not ready for this, and so initially considered declining. However, since I was going to get to *keep* my M-16 by my side, I found my hand raising. The Colonel must have seen something in me, as he pretty much hand-picked all of his "special assignment" soldiers. I accepted, and then the Colonel personally told me that he was very happy, as he *needed* me and had hoped I would volunteer. I would have done anything for that Colonel!

Camp Evans was almost too quiet, and had been the location of much bloodshed many times in the past. The Colonel helped to set up about fifteen to twenty of us from Personnel, Procurement, Finance, etc., and I was with a completely new group of men, although I may have seen some of the other soldiers before, from a distance, back at Camp Campbell. Before he left, the Colonel made sure that we had all we needed.

Although I was still very shy and not very good at speaking in front of people, I had the "first station" set up and ready to go right as the soldiers from the field were entering. I briefed them on what to expect in their two to three days of processing-through.

> **I could see the look of many battles on the faces of the soldiers of the 101st.**
>
> **Some of the men were partially bandaged up, some still had dirty faces, and some**
>
> **had uncombed hair. They all had darkened skin from exposure**
>
> **to the rain, sun, gun grease, and grime of war.**
>
> **They were uniformly quiet, respectful, and they had seen a lot of action.**
>
> ***These were America's best.***

I decided that all of this explaining and processing-through would give me a really great practice opportunity at public speaking, and I was determined to become better at providing the "Orientation Overview" to the next group. Again, the men were very cordial and they knew I was doing my best to do my job, although I was not "a natural." I credit the Army for giving me a job where I could *work through one of my major deficiencies: public speaking.* I knew this was holding me back from future work, after Vietnam, and I needed to work on it. Well, as it turns out, I worked on it for many decades!

At Camp Evans, I was glad to be by myself again in my sleeping quarters, and I do not remember any required bunker guard duty on this short assignment. I slept in the out-processing area upstairs and had the whole floor to myself for a while.

With the new younger group of soldiers now working back in the Personnel Branch, I was glad to be more on my own and just responsible for me. I remember drinking only a half-can of beer that entire month I was up at Camp Evans and *that* gave me a headache.

I wanted out of Vietnam and my tour was coming to an end. I did not want any screw-ups by me or others to get in the way. I had been a pretty good soldier, but when you get complacent, like in the Watchtower, then, when you least expect it, you can get *killed.*

I enjoyed the solitude and time for reading and reflection after work, as the guys stopped processing through around 5:00 p.m. It was a good time to try to decompress and just enjoy this new job, which I kept working hard to be better at. Nobody was doing drugs, stealing my *Cokes*, sticking their hands in fans, spreading rumors to mess with us, or shooting Sergeants, so I thought that I had *a better chance of surviving up by the DMZ!* I would make that move again today, if given the choice.

Thanksgiving came and went while I was at Camp Evans, but I do not remember sadness, or anything like that, at not being able to go anywhere. I did, however, feel nostalgia for the Green Bay Packers and Detroit Lions "Turkey Day Game" that had been played annually when I was a child. But, I was alive and I had made a positive choice for safety! Years later in Washington, DC, when I "felt" that I was expected to visit family and friends—if I didn't go out—then sadness would set in for hours.

The short assignment at Camp Evans ended as promised, and I returned back to Camp Campbell.

It wasn't until *after* I returned home to the States that I found out that the *entire 101st* was pulled out of Vietnam on March 10, 1972—some *nine weeks* after I left!

Then, on March 30, 1972, with the "Eastertide Offensive," the VC marched across the DMZ and assaulted Quang Tri Province. Without "me" and the 101st at Phu Bai, it was easy for the VC! It shocked me how close I had come to the "end."

Now I fully understand why we were rushed into action at Camp Evans!

I have always hoped that *Ike* left his seat in the latrine and got home. Maybe that's the reason I can't locate him.

CHAPTER 26

"Out'a Here!"

I look back at some of the pictures of me later on in my tour in 1971, and I can see how the War had worn me down with the stress and uncertainty. We all got worn down, and it was not from the work, and it did not happen right away for most of us.

But the effects of the War were apparent on our faces.

I do not remember the guys we replaced at the front of the year looking so tired.

Not exactly "partying."

My buddy Gary, heading out for bunker guard duty, with our hootch seen in the background. Our new puppy is in the lower left of the picture. (NOTE: The white on the ground is SAND . . . not snow.)

**This is the last picture I have of Brutus and me,
taken in front of my hootch at Camp Campbell toward the end of my tour.
The cameraman encouraged me to smile,
but even Brutus appears worn down.**

I was now going into my last full month and had almost made it through in one piece! But I was *worn down* from the War, the smell of gun powder, of burning human waste and diesel fuel, of the incoming rockets and mortar attacks, the rain, the cultural difference, the drab terrain, and … I missed home.

As talked about earlier, this is a "Short-Timer's Calendar." We were able to cross out each day of the last months, accordingly, up to and including our "last day" in Vietnam. There were many versions, and this is one of the most "innocent." Courtesy of Randy Parmley.

It is paradoxical that when you are sometimes given time to think and reflect, you return to a situation, *hating it more.* I thought often of a letter written by my Father during World War II. It had been sent to me by my Uncle Roman (who was also my Godfather), and, as my Tour was coming to an end, I understood more fully the emotions, and the *mood* it transmitted.

"Leyte" Phillipine Its.   Tues. 1:32 P.M.
                            Sept. 18. 45

Dearest Brother:-

Well it's about time Im writing you a few lines, or trying to print you might say. Oh for the day when Letter Writing will come to the end. That will be when I'm on the way home. & I just heard a good news broadcast don't be surprised if I drop in on you all one of these days, you'd better have some good ligour on tap. How's everything at home Brown & please take the best care of Mom. Pleased to hear she made the trip to Va. okay and that Leo is coming along. May I get to see him soon.

ARE many of the boys home on Discharge as yet. I can't understand how Pinhook is back in the Army. My best Regards to Sam D, John G. And all the rest that are home.

Darn it if it doesn't rain six out of seven days in Leyte. & hot weather in between. To help pass the time away Im going back to good old school days again. & remember how we used to love

-2-

To GO TO School. I'M TAKING TYPING, ELECTRICITY
+ SMALL BUSINESS, ONE THING IT CAN'T DO
ME ANY hARM.

How's The OLD HOMESTEAD COMING ALONG
I IMAGINE YOUR STILL IMPROVING The PLACE
ThAT IS IN YOUR SPARE TIME. I WOULD
SURE LOVE TO SEE The PLACE AGAIN. BROWN
NOT ThAT I DON'T WANT TO WRITE TO YOU
MORE OFTEN, but I CONSIDER ThAT WHEN
I WRITE TO MOM, WELL IT'S TO YOU ALSO.
O.K.

ALL YOU HEAR AROUND HERE "WHEN
AM I GOING HOME" WELL I CAN'T BLAME
THEM FOR ThAT. The damm ThING IS ALL
OVER NOW AND ThANK GOD IVE GOT MY
HEALTH AND GOD BLESS The MORE UNFORTUNATE
ONES. but The OLD SAYING WAR IS BITTER.
WELL BROWN I'LL CLOSE FOR Today
AND WILL WRITE AGAIN SOON. & TILL
ThEN Keep The HomeFires BuRNING.
MY BEST Regards To ALL.

BROTHER
"Joseph"

SGT. J.R. CHESKAWICH.
BTRY "C" 223 F.A. BN. A.P.O. 72
% POST MASTER SAN FRANSISCO
CALIF. U.S. ARMY

AIR MAIL

MR. ROMAN G. CHESKAWICH
BOX 35
BUNOLA
PENNSYLVANIA.

CHAPTER 27

Bob Hope Brings

"The Hope of the Holidays" To Us

During this last month of my tour, the story circulated that another one of our soldiers had died in a helicopter accident on his way out of Camp Campbell to an airport that was to take him back to the U.S. That was upsetting, as his time was up and he got killed returning home. It was not fair, but then war and life are "that way"—even if that phrase does not make it easier to take. To brighten things up and to give us something to look forward to, the Episcopalian minister was looking for volunteers to sing in the choir for Christmas Eve service. Choir practice started a few weeks before Christmas and we were given time off to practice. There were eight or ten of us in the group.

At some point, just before Christmas, "The Bob Hope Christmas Tour" came to our Base and we *were grateful that he and all of those with him <u>cared enough</u> to come to the War to entertain us.* Soldiers in the 101st came to Phu Bai from throughout the "I Corps" to see Bob Hope, Vida Blue, "Les Brown and His Band of Renown," and the "Miss America Court." *We were not disappointed.* It was a warm day and some of us took off our tee-shirts and Fatigue jackets as we sat in the amphitheater on wooden benches.

When I look at these snapshots now, I am in awe that the young women in the "Miss America" group were so open and sharing, and so full of life and fun....After all, they, too, like us, had never seen a war-torn country, or been so far from home and at risk *themselves*, and yet *they brought home and normalcy* to us.

I think about the fact that Bob Hope, as a living icon of self-sacrifice and dedication to American troops throughout the world, surely could have been a "target" for the North Vietnamese (and surely, also, to our enemies, during his World War II performances). His "name" and his schedule were both always open to the public.

My thanks also go to Vida Blue, Les Brown and his band members, and all of the other celebrities and staff throughout the years. They all did their part.

Christmas Eve arrived and our small choir sang well at the Episcopalian service. I remember one of the songs we worked on that has since become my favorite, *O Holy Night.* There was no planned Catholic Mass for Christmas so I did the best I could.

On the way back to the hootch a little after Midnight, I faintly saw and smelled

smoke coming through the screens. I opened up the screen door and was greeted by more smoke! I found the source of the fire quickly and woke everyone up. The soldier from The Great Lakes area had been drinking, fell asleep, and the bare bulb of his lamp had fallen onto his pillow—which was on fire…as well as his hair and shirt. He was zonked out in a deep drunken stupor. We put out the fire by throwing the pillow outside and dousing it with water, and by simultaneously throwing water on the guy to stop his shirt and hair from burning. I believe I threw more water than I needed to at his face to wake him up.

If I had not been out at church singing—and I am not even Episcopalian—we could have all gone up in flames within a few minutes! We told him what we thought of his behavior that night, and again the next day, to reinforce his unacceptable behavior. We never reported him, as that is not what buddies do, but we razzed him for days.

On Christmas morning, the Episcopalian minster said we were all needed back at the chapel for an "encore performance," as a Two-Star General was in camp. I remember shaking hands with the General and turning a bright red...like Rudolph's nose.

Since I had spent almost a month at Camp Evans with soldiers from Procurement, Finance, and Supplies, it was easier now to talk with them in the Mess Hall, during breaks, after formation, or at the PX as we had something in common. A few of us got to thinking what it would take to process someone out of Phu Bai to go back home, and wondered why it took weeks, when we all worked together and just had to figure out what was needed.

Three of us asked one of the officers in charge. We were told that the processing-out time period was "unpredictable" and usually started two to three weeks before the 12-month tour period was over.

We asked him, "Why does it take so long?"

He told us, "Well, it's because of all the clearances needed, and the long lines each day to obtain approval stamps and initials from each component." He continued, "So, you see, one day is allotted for each clearance point needed."

We asked, "Could anyone get out if they only served 11-1/2 months, but had all the clearances?"

"Yes, sure," he replied. "If he was cleared, he could leave." But he added, shaking his head, "It is pretty unlikely that this could happen."

That was all we needed to hear! We did not need Peter Drucker, the famous management guru, or some MBA, to tell us what to *do!* The three of us decided to try.

Another day in Vietnam is another day risking your life that the "Grim Reaper" will find you! No one is certain of anything in war and we had just been given "tacit permission" to figure out a way.

I learned a lesson here, which is *to just keep asking questions!* Just because something has not been done before, that does not make it impossible. I figured this lesson would also stand me in good stead once I got out of Vietnam and into the work world.

The three of us worked with our connections and obtained *all* of our own clearances, as everything was in order! We were so effective that I think we could have gotten even Humphrey Bogart out of *Casablanca* within his first month in town…but, then, there would have been no need for the movie.

Still, I was not about to risk taking anything out of the War that did not belong to me or that I had not earned.

On the day for my "lift off" by helicopter, I talked with the Sergeant in the morning who told me that if I was willing to stay two more weeks, until mid-January, which was the anniversary of my one year in Vietnam, I would get promoted to Specialist 5, E-5. I told him "thank you," but since everything was *"cleared,"* I was going on the helicopter *today* to catch the "Big Bird" to the mainland.

I remember saying "Goodbye" to the guys quickly, and the rumor monger quickly told me that it was just as well I was leaving, as he saw more and more awful things going on…. "For example, just this morning…."

That was enough of this "hotshot" with his stories, so I smiled, brushed him off, and ran with my head down for the helicopter!

One of the other guys who had also gotten his clearances boarded the helicopter with me. The other fellow changed his mind and waited out two more weeks until his year was up. I have always hoped he made it out.

CHAPTER 28

Well, Not So Fast....

"Agent Orange," The Gift That Keeps On Giving

Most Vets will argue that the conservative Veterans Administration (VA) has been late in recognizing the *Agent Orange* carcinogenic effects, but it did come around. With taxpayer dollars at stake, the VA could not be anything but conservative.

I had started working in the Personnel Branch in Phu Bai during the cool season in January 1971 when the temperature seldom dropped below 60-degrees Fahrenheit and did not go above 70-degrees Fahrenheit. I remember the light drizzle and the humidity which built up to the summer and monsoon season. Camp Campbell, the headquarters for the 101st Airborne Division, was spread out over hundreds of acres and included an Air Force Base, among other military attachments.

Some of us had asked our superiors very early in our Tour about *"Agent Orange"* and we were told the area and adjacent areas had not been sprayed for a year and a half and so we had nothing to worry about, as it had all "dried up."

Agent Orange, which contains Dioxin, a carcinogen, was one of several chemicals dropped from C-123 Air Force planes to "defoliate" the trees and vegetation so that the Viet Cong could be more readily "observed" when using the Ho Chi Minh Trail, which bordered western South Vietnam with Laos and Cambodia. There were other chemicals dropped in the large scale military operation which was termed "Operation Ranch Hand." The *"Agent Orange"* designation came about because of the band of color-coding on the outside of the drums containing the chemical.

We have learned much about the effects of *Agent Orange* over the last forty-five years, including that it has a half-life of 11–15 years in the human body, and has been shown to cause cancer in humans, in addition to a host of other presumptive conditions Vietnam Veterans are showing up with, years after exposure—through the water, air, food supply chain, or through contact with the skin.

In my case, the prostate cancer did not present itself until I was almost 60 years old. I have not read too much about what the spraying has done to the Vietnamese population but I have my own theory. I do not think any country can use anything similar to *Agent Orange* for the same purposes ever again. **Yes, we met the legal test at the time as it was…a defoliant… but we have learned a lot since then.**

I remember Camp Campbell as mostly brown and dusty. But photographs from the time I served show green grass, too. *Agent Orange* did kill the leaves on the trees that were sprayed along the Trail, and we now know that the environmental effect can take years, even decades, to show up from water run-off affecting humans, vegetation, and wildlife.

I remember the rice paddies, water buffalo, and Vietnamese workers—most of whom were women—and I wonder. . . .

The Democratic Republic of Vietnam. Peasants of a village in the Quang Binh Province tilling a rice field. (The Image Works, NY)

CHAPTER 29

Goodbye, Vietnam

Like most of us in the U.S., I have seen the popular films of the Vietnam War stories and its Vets. Most of it is pretty gruesome stuff, and it has often left me with *flashbacks* and *tortured dreams*. I never met anyone "over there" who collected sliced-off enemy ears, played dangerous games with a rifle or pistol, massacred Vietnamese babies and children, assaulted women, collected a truck load of AK-47's to take back to the U.S., or talked back to officers, as Robin Williams did in *Good Morning, Vietnam*.

I was not an officer in Vietnam, but I was appalled at the portrayal of Adrian Cronauer as a renegade, out-of-control Armed Forces radio announcer, who could pretty much do as he pleased. I felt badly for the Air Force officers depicted in the movie, and I would never have tolerated that behavior if I had been a supervisor!

We did have *fragging* of officers in Vietnam from War accounts, and some of it may have happened with greater frequency as the War dragged on, but I was not aware of any cases except the one instance in the 101st Administrative Company where a soldier purportedly shot and killed the Sergeant on our camp perimeter bunker line.

I am sure we had our "John Rambo" types in Vietnam but I don't know any war stories personally of men like those who were represented in the Hollywood movies by Sylvester Stallone and Chuck Norris on their respective suicidal missions. I can, however, identify with large parts of *The Deer Hunter* since, I went deer hunting on my uncle's farm in Indiana, Pennsylvania soon after returning from Vietnam, shot and missed a buck, worked in the U.S. Steel plant in Clairton, Pennsylvania (which was the small town setting for the movie), and attended a Polish wedding on my immediate return from Vietnam in January 1972.

Although I did not look anything like Robert De Nero in the movie, I also could be moody. I was "jumpy," too, and that stayed with me many, many years. I could not just

turn it off. If I could have figured out how, I would surely have done it a long time ago.

One of our returning Vets from Afghanistan (and a former student in the Battle Ground, WA school area) asked me, during the summer of 2013, when being on *High Alert* stops after returning home. I suggested that he contact a confidential counselor, and that he also contact the VA to let them know that he was "home," so that he could get into their "system." That way, he could get physical and medical testings and follow-up care.

Still, most of what has been fed through the media has been *negative stereotyping* of the Vietnam Veteran. We were not all druggies and alcoholics, either while "In-Country" or after Service for the rest of our lives.

It was a different war than Americans were used to, although the Civil War with Stonewall Jackson attacking, retreating, and choosing when to engage was difficult for the North to understand also at the time. The soldiers did not always know who the enemy was in that war, either.

As I walked up the stair-landing to the plane that was to carry me home, I turned back for an instant to look at what was soon to be behind me: Although I was trained to kill, and had entered Bien Hoa/Long Binh, South Vietnam in January 1971 as an Infantryman, I would soon be a civilian, again.

> **It had been a sacrifice**
> **and an obligation to serve**
> **...and I was a survivor.**

PART THREE

Homecoming

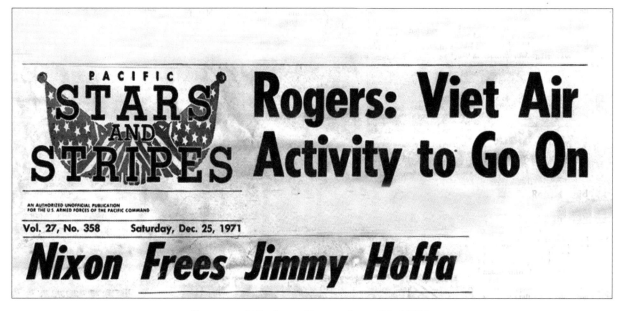

Stars and Stripes, December 25, 1971.

CHAPTER 30

On the "Big Bird"…Coming Home

I was finally out of the War and Vietnam.

I thought that Vietnam was going to be out of my mind quickly! We toasted New Year's Eve and Day on the plane ride back. Sitting in my airplane seat, I read the Sports Section and noted that Penn State had defeated Texas in the January 1, 1972 "Cotton Bowl," as Franco Harris and Lydell Mitchell were both in the backfield in Penn State's 30-6 win. Some things had not changed and that was good.

I also read more again about this new-concept television show called *All In the Family* created by Norman Lear. I could not wait to get home to see what all the commotion had been about for the past nine months or so.

I remember when the plane landed at Sea-Tac Airport in Washington State,
I knelt down and kissed the black asphalt,
as I was glad to be back on U.S. ground.
Australia was very friendly, but this was my country.
There was no celebration with a band, nor were there any dancing girls.
No one welcomed me and the other returning soldiers back.
But, maybe, better than that, there were no protesters
calling me a "Pig" or "Baby Killer."
I look back and personally do not feel bad about
the lack of a welcoming committee.

To be honest, I do not want a party…even now. I did not want one then.
It is possible most of us feel this way.

We served, we sacrificed,
and now we had to move to the next step.

"THE KID IS COMING HOME"

(Sanitized version)

THIS____DAY OF_____, 19__

TO: _____

VERY SOON, **Jim Cheskawich** WILL ONCE AGAIN BE IN YOUR MIDST, DE-AMERICANIZED, DEMORALIZED, AND DEHYDRATED, BUT READY ONCE MORE TO TAKE HIS PLACE AS A HUMAN BEING TO ENGAGE IN LIFE, LIBERTY, AND A SOMEWHAT DELAYED PURSUIT OF HAPPINESS.

IN MAKING YOUR JOYOUS PREPARATIONS TO WELCOME HIM BACK INTO RESPECTABLE SOCIETY ONCE AGAIN, YOU MUST MAKE ALLOWANCES FOR THE CRUDE ENVIRONMENT IN WHICH HE HAS SUFFERED FOR THE PAST 12 MONTHS. IN A WORD, HE MAY BE SOMEWHAT ... SUFFERING THE "VIET CONG-ITIS" OR PERHAPS HUNG-OVER FROM DRINKING TOO MUCH WARM XXXX BRAND BEER THESE PAST 12 MONTHS.

THEREFORE, SHOW NO ALARM IF HE PREFERS TO SQUAT RATHER THAN SIT ON A CHAIR. SHOW NOT A HINT OF SURPRISE IF HE INSISTS ON SLINGING HIS WEAPON AT THE DINNER TABLE OR WAKES YOU IN THE MIDDLE OF THE NIGHT TO PULL YOUR GUARD. MAINTAIN YOUR COOL AS YOU WATCH HIM POUR GRAVY ON HIS DESSERT. PRETEND NOT TO NOTICE WHEN HE EATS WITH HIS FINGERS INSTEAD OF YOUR BEST SILVER, OR PREFERS CANNED GOODS TO A JUICY STEAK. MAKE EVERY ATTEMPT TO FORCE A SMILE WHEN HE TAKES YOUR BEST BLANKET OFF THE BED AND SPREADS IT OUT ON THE GROUND TO SLEEP.

IF IT SHOULD START RAINING, PAY NO ATTENTION IF HE PULLS OFF HIS CLOTHES, GRABS A BAR OF SOAP, AND RUNS OUTDOORS TO TAKE A SHOWER. IGNORE HIS FASCINATION WITH RUNNING WATER. MERELY SMILE AT HIS SIMPLENESS, FOR EVENTUALLY THE NOVELTY OF THESE THINGS WILL WEAR OFF.

ANY OF THESE THINGS SHOULD BE AVOIDED, AS THEY CAN PRODUCE A STATE OF ADVANCED SHOCK: PEOPLE DANCING...CHILDREN WITH TOY GRENADES ...WOMEN...AND A FULL CASE OF XXX

BRAND BEER. IN A RELATIVELY SHORT TIME, HIS PROFANITY WILL DECREASE ENOUGH TO PERMIT HIM TO ASSOCIATE WITH MIXED GROUPS, AND SOON HE WILL BE SPEAKING A RECOGNIZABLE FORM OF ENGLISH. FOR A WHILE, HE MAY COMPLAIN ABOUT SLEEPING ON A SPRING MATTRESS AND AT FIRST MAY REFUSE TO GO TO BED WITHOUT A MOSQUITO NET.

NEVER ASK WHY THE JONES' BOY HELD A HIGHER RANK THAN HE DID, AND BY NO MEANS MENTION THE TERM "RE UP." PRETEND NOT TO NOTICE IF AT A RESTAURANT HE CALLS A WAITRESS A NUMBER ONE . . . AND USES HIS HAT AS AN ASHTRAY. HE WILL PROBABLY KEEP LISTENING FOR "COMING HOME SOLDIER" TO PLAY ON THE RADIO OR "WE GOT TO GET OUT OF THIS PLACE."

FOR THE FIRST FEW MONTHS, UNTIL HE IS HOUSEBROKEN, BE ESPECIALLY WATCHFUL SHOULD HE BE PLACED IN THE COMPANY OF A WOMAN, PARTICULARLY ONE WHO IS YOUNG AND BEAUTIFUL . . . HIS FIRST REACTION MAY BE TO GO INTO A CATATONIC SHOCK. TAKE ADVANTAGE OF THIS MOMENTARY HESITATION AND MOVE THE YOUNG LADY OUT OF HIS REACH.

KEEP IN MIND THAT BENEATH THAT TANNED AND RUGGED EXTERIOR THERE STILL BEATS A HEART OF PURE GOLD. TREASURE THIS, FOR IT IS ABOUT THE ONLY THING OF VALUE THAT HE HAS LEFT. TREAT HIM WITH KINDNESS, TOLERANCE, AND AN OCCASIONAL FIFTH OF GOOD WHISKEY, AND YOU WILL SOON BE ABLE TO REHABILITATE THIS HOLLOW SHELL OF THE MAN YOU ONCE KNEW.

SEND NO MORE MAIL TO VIETNAM AFTER TODAY.

FILL THE ICEBOX WITH BEER, GET THE CIVIES OUT OF THE MOTHBALLS, FILL THE CAR WITH GAS, AND GET THE WOMEN AND CHILDREN OFF THE STREETS!!!

THE KID IS COMING HOME. . . .

IN WITNESS WHEREOF THE PARTY OF THE FIRST PART HAS EXECUTED THIS WARNING AND SET HIS HAND HEREUNTO:

/S/ _____ **Jim Cheskawich** _____

CHAPTER 31

Home Again

———————————————

I stayed at Ft. Lewis, Washington for a few days and processed-through. The theme in the Army universally is, "Hurry up and wait." I remember noting "for the record" that I had "hearing difficulty around loud noises," but I have never used hearing aids to this day and just work around the problem. (The humming and hissing sounds, now, go in and out.)

In the background, Don McLean's *American Pie* was playing almost hourly on someone's radio, or so it seemed, while I went through my processing-out clearance points—which seemed like it *might* take two weeks!

During my processing-through, one of the officers offered me several Stateside assignment options IF I stayed on for six more months…the chance for another promotion to Specialist E-5 (which I already walked away from in Vietnam) and more GI-benefits to go to college. I responded that I already had my B.S. Degree and did not need any more college. If I could "get out now," that was my preference and I did not need another promotion.

I did want to go home and rebuild my life.

We both agreed that I was eligible to separate as I had just come out of Vietnam and served a full tour over there. He appeared disappointed in my decision, but if it was doable, I wanted out, as my turn at bat had been served. I used to think that I served eighteen months in the Service but, from early August 1970 until the first week in January 1972 is only seventeen months. Once I knew what I wanted, I usually moved quickly ... and getting my clearances in as timely a manner as possible was no exception.

I stayed in a hotel in Seattle for three days before I took a flight back to Pittsburgh. I knew that I needed some time to myself and I just wanted to sleep and go to three to four movies every day.

I do not remember any of the movies I saw. It did not matter, as I was back in the U.S. My Sony radio got left behind on the sidewalk in Seattle as the taxi driver loaded up my duffel bag in the trunk of the taxi as I sat upfront waiting for the ride to Sea-Tac Airport. That is probably why, if possible, I still like *to do things myself,* as I know they will be done, or I can only blame myself.

On the flight back, I recall listening to The Doors singing *Riders on the Storm* over the airplane headphones. This song turned out to be *prophetic*…as I was riding into a *sure storm* by going home and being *unsure of my future.*

I realize that the recording also could have been about going into Vietnam, but Jim Morrison had not recorded it until mid-1971 when I was already "In-Country."

 I have to admit that a part of me did not want to go straight home. *Home was going to be different, and I certainly had changed.* I had nowhere else to go, so I did what was expected of me.

When I arrived back in the Pittsburgh area, everyone was at a cousin's wedding in Indiana, Pennsylvania. I did not tell them I was coming and just drove up in uniform. As in the scene from *The Deer Hunter,* "the Pennsylvania boy" was truly *welcomed* back home! I enjoyed myself at the Polish wedding celebration, and told everyone I was getting a job as soon as I could with my B.S. in Management.

I returned home after the wedding and realized pretty quickly that a lot of things seemed different.

The War was supposed to be "over" for me. I had made it back in one piece, but I was *anxious* and *could not relax.* Looking back, the VA or Department of Defense (DOD) should have been checking on me every day or week to make sure I was making a successful transition without a lot of "self-medication." Some guys do not make the transition completely. You are trained to kill, get sent to a war, get shot at, witness some extremes of human behavior, and are then expected to turn it off and forget all that as you try to mainstream as soon as you return!

I do not think it can be done, at least not with my make-up.

I even told my Mom a few times that she made me nervous.

That was bold, and hurtful, of me! But, of course, "I" was the problem.

Once, my brother Bernie brushed my elbow while we were fixing the insides of our old white Plymouth Valiant, and I snapped back quickly, **"Don't touch me!"**

I started staying up late, reaching out to my old friends to have a drink with, and began to sleep in until the afternoon hours.

I was starting to slide.

I looked through the Want Ads for jobs and made a few visits to the employment/ unemployment offices in the Pittsburgh area, but it was a tough time to find a job. I ran out of things to do at home and thought I just wanted to be busy doing something useful. Still, however, a part of me did not know what I wanted to do.

CHAPTER 32

Post-War College-Daze

After being home a few weeks, I went back up to Penn State to visit and found myself wandering toward the Admissions Office for graduate school. I had not planned on graduate school as a goal. It was winter time and that campus gets pretty cold trying to deal with wind and blowing snow. The walk across the parking lot in East Halls in a February snowstorm could overcome a student and they would not be found until the April thaw! I needed something to do and did not feel like staying outside much longer so I went into a few buildings before I went to Recreation (Rec) Hall to play basketball. Then I saw the Graduate School Admissions Office. Why would I want to go in *there*?

I inquired about the MBA program and was told I could begin in March/April of 1972 as an adjunct student and would have to do well in my business grad school classes and also on the Admission Test for Graduate Studies in Business (ATGSB) or I was just wasting everyone's time. The G.I. Bill would pay for my grad school education. I was told it was a long shot and probably not worth the risk, but I went ahead and took the application and began preparing to start grad school an unbelievable *three months* after leaving Vietnam. I was tired of watching Johnny Carson most nights of the week and knew I had to be doing something, anything ... even grad school!

I had a goal *now*, and I was going to make it!

"Old Main," Penn State

Over at Rec Hall that afternoon and early evening, the recent Pittsburgh Steelers #1 draft pick and future NFL Hall of Famer Franco Harris was in a pick-up "5-on-5" basketball game. Another player was needed so I joined in and got run over twice by the opposing team's center. I did not even take a contested rebound as Franco, who was born in Ft. Dix, New Jersey, always cleared the boards. He was also a very good basketball player. But I could still take a hit and I did not have padding like some of those linebackers he ran over for thirteen years. Later on, he learned to appreciate another Spec 4 Vietnam Veteran, Rocky Bleier, who served as his lead blocker on the way to winning *four* "Super Bowls" with the Steelers!

During the early part of 1972 while waiting for grad school to start, I reconnected with my old roommate, Tom (whose Dad had attended Louisiana State University on a football scholarship) from my undergraduate days at Penn State. He was working at the Armed Forces Entrance and Examination Station in Pittsburgh. He had enlisted for three years and chose his own military occupational specialty and duty station.

Tom seemed to be doing well, but the first thing he said when he saw me was, "You're *different!*"

I told him about my plans for grad school and he probably reminded me of how I did not take some of my Management courses all that seriously as an undergrad, but...that if I could go to grad school, so could he! I still remember his laugh! That was all the encouragement I needed.

Tom would have done very well in grad school but it did not interest him. I was *"different"* though, now, and he knew it. More focused, more energy, but sometimes too much energy.

How was I going to stay calm? It was not meant to be for many, many years, but I did my best.

Grad school started for me and I had a full load of classes as the government was paying my tuition on the GI Bill. I took the Admission Test for Graduate Studies in Business (ATGSB), and, unlike the Armed Forces Entrance Exam, I did my best, as Penn State was not going to put me on the front line to get shot, like a newly minted Officer Candidate School Second Lieutenant as a reward for testing well. Sometimes, I feel guilty about not doing my best on the Armed Forces Entrance Exam but I had a good reason: *to survive.* I scored very well on the ATGSB and the score in itself could have gotten me into a number of highly rated Business grad schools, but I was a "Penn Stater" and could not go anywhere else.

I certainly needed comfortable and familiar surroundings as I had my "War issues" … which I admitted to no one.

I was accepted the next term into the MBA program and my course work as an "adjunct student" counted. My plan was to max out on courses and finish grad school in five (10 week) terms, which is what happened. I received my MBA in June 1973. Looking back, I could not have been thinking too clearly, as I set myself up for a lot of class work and I still had the War fresh in my mind.

I hit the books very hard and remember reading those Management text books with Koss Pro-4A headphones listening to Tchaikovsky's *1812 Overture,* Beethoven's *5th Symphony,* Schubert's *Unfinished Symphony,* Dvorak's *From the New World* Symphony, Rod Stewart, The Temptations, Jethro Tull, or Janis Joplin, as I ate dinner and drank to "self-medicate," while Paul, one of my roommates, had his TEAC tape-deck on, playing John Denver and Michael, my other roommate, was watching the New York Rangers hockey feed. The Rangers seemed to be always playing.

Folks wonder how I can handle a full Kindergarten class at age 68, but I had my "basic training" a long time ago with a lot of activity going on at once. I just needed to be in *control* (or at least *feel* that way), which helped me with some of the after-War stress.

Sometimes my two roommates and I would go downtown for dinner and drinks, or to a party with other students in our Beaver Terrace apartment complex, which was just a ten-minute walk from the Main Campus.

Mike liked to sing at the Phyrst Bar and Restaurant, but I just could not get into it. It just was not me.

I never quite felt I could enjoy myself and I would ask myself why? Something had been taken from me in the War. It is just a "something" that each Vet comes to know about and maybe is not so hard for some to explain. It is a small sadness or hole in our make-up that is just there. Until you have been "there," it is hard to understand.

I could not think, hear, or talk over the loud music and noise anyway so I usually kept quiet whenever we went out. Over time, the hearing with background noise became a problem, but that is what happens when you have a helicopter landing and takeoff port behind your *desk!* As for the lack of hearing, it is better than coming back with a missing limb or limbs so, although I get frustrated, it could be a lot worse.

One late weekend night during the summer term, I was sitting with other students on the wall down the hill from Old Main and on College Avenue.

An elderly gentleman stopped by. He looked at me and asked, "Is anything *wrong,* young man?"

I must have been thinking of what I had left behind in Vietnam…and I was determined that <u>no one</u> was *ever* going to see *that* in my *face* again!

Sometimes, I felt guilty about not being on patrol in Vietnam and getting shot-at every few days, like the other guys I trained with, who served their entire tours as Infantrymen. But then, I only used my skills and talents—which I had been given—to always be looking to improve my position, thus enhancing my survival odds.

I did feel that somehow I shortchanged my fellow friends in that I had made it out and in one piece, and they didn't. *Why me?* **Survivors feel guilt, too.**

So, here, I was, now, in grad school, doing well in class, and thinking that others were still over there, and how could I or anyone be truly happy knowing what a mess it was in Vietnam?

Why should I be the lucky one and escape the madness?

I was a bit "nervous" and "jumpy," but I figured that this would pass over much time and I would learn to relax and not be doing something to *just keep busy.* There was a Veterans' group at Penn State but, of course, I thought I did not *need* them and I would go on my *own.* I think we had one other Veteran in the MBA program, but I kept my "Service experiences" to myself.

One weekend evening around 2:30 a.m. as a few of us were leaving downtown to go back to our rooms, a group of "townies" showed up in an open-bed truck with several guys swinging chains. One guy made a statement to the effect that we were "all worthless." Then he said, "There's not a *man* among you!"

I stepped forward to challenge him, and he swung a tire chain at me, but somehow the driver of the truck pulled away at that exact moment and there was no damage to anyone. The friends I had come back with wisely wanted no part of this as we were outnumbered 8-to-3 and we did not have chains, or a truck.

I did not back down but I soon realized that this was pretty stupid on my part. I was out of the War maybe a year now, but still I was trained to *kill.* Of that, I had no doubt. From that incident, I decided I was not going to respond with *anger* so quickly in the future.

I then began to just go into a *passive* mode whenever confrontations or disagreements came up. I knew that I had to control my temper or I was going to hurt someone. *I was a trained killer.*

Usually, I was pretty good for the next few decades about not losing it. But, sometimes, I stood up to people or situations in unexpected ways, and—as I look back—I did not know where that came from.

Only *now*, I have my suspicions.

"GS" (General Schedule) Levels
and
Military Rank Equivalencies

(Geneva Convention Categories)

Although civilian "GS" (General Schedule) workers do not have military rank, government regulations include civilian and military "Grade Equivalencies" for pay and for protocol-comparison purposes. For example, a "GS-9" is considered comparable to a First Lieutenant, while a "GS-15" (top of the scale, *and I attained this*) is the *equivalent* Grade of a Full Colonel. Senior Executive Service (SES) and Senior Grade Equivalencies were created by the U.S. Department of Defense for the purpose of treating civilians serving alongside the Armed Forces, who have been captured as Prisoners of War, according to the "Geneva Convention."

SOURCE: U.S. Department of Defense, 1974.

CHAPTER 33

Working For the Feds

After graduation in 1973, I was again faced with the poor job market in Pittsburgh that was reflecting the long-term decline in domestic steel-making and related industries. I worked as a management consultant for three weeks right after grad school. I did not have the classroom skills, and I certainly did not have, at the time, the experience of working in the "real world" as a professional. By mutual agreement, the job ended. Of course, I was depressed over this and continued with my self-medication.

After being unemployed for six months, I then drove a vacuum truck with 15-gears (two gear boxes) for a company in Duquesne, PA. I was not told about the second gear box which had "Low, Medium, High" or "L, M, H," respectively, and one night I nearly wiped out half the town of Duquesne on my long trip from the mill *up the hill* to the company's garage! It is almost a 45-degree hill. The truck kept drifting back at stop signs and red lights and I had to take a side street, get a good running start, and hope I did not have to stop that sucker! Had I put the truck in "L," instead of keeping it in "M," I would not have taken 45-minutes to make a one mile trip. Of course, now-a-days, you have to pass a truck-driving *test* before they give you the keys to a truck that I should *never* have been driving. I probably lost five pounds on that ride. Fortunately, it was around Midnight on a week night and no one was on the road. I think the truck weighed 90,000 pounds, empty. It was substantial and could have done a lot of damage if it drifted back down the hill too far—with me in the cab. I began to think that I might not have had it so bad, after all, with Vietnam and the machine gun fire when I was in the Watchtower!

I picked up a "snuff and chewing tobacco" habit from my Mill buddies, as I was not allowed to smoke my pipe in the Mills. That awful habit stayed with me through several girlfriends and about fifteen years. It did calm my nerves but it was a very addicting habit.

I had kept *silent* about my MBA and my Vietnam Service. At one point, the men asked me to be their designated union representative but I said, "No." I was in one of the best jobs I ever had in my life as we seldom saw the boss.

Over the last few years, we have now followed through the media the stories of job seekers and fired managers, coaches, businessmen, and political office holders who have indicated on their resumes that they "Served in Vietnam." We even have "stolen valor" cases of false medal claims. Now, it looks like enough time has passed that it is considered "respectable" to *admit* to Vietnam or Vietnam era service.

"If you can make it in *Vietnam* and get out of there without too much damage, you can probably make it anywhere." We used to hear this said about growing up and surviving in *New York*. But I never heard of anyone typing on their resume that they "spent a year in New York" and that, somehow, this was going to mean the same thing as "one year in Vietnam."

I remember after I got my first job offer in Washington, DC, and I told everyone I was leaving. One of the laborers put the heavy lid on the 15-foot sewer entrance *after* he took up the ladder. The walls were lined with stinking sewage, and I was unable to climb more than three feet off the bottom. I screamed from down there for "Help!" and—after 20-minutes—another Mill worker got me out of there.

The guy who had tried to leave me in the sewer was unapologetic.

He said, "You have been *lying* to everyone! You pretended like you were unemployable and minimally educated, like you're willing to do whatever it takes to make a living. And now we find out that you have just been killing time, waiting for a cushy government job!"

I tried to reason with him. "Look, I needed a job just like everyone else. This is a good job, and I have been grateful for it."

You have to fit in with your peers and what he had done was wrong. I chose to just walk away. I would not have wanted him in *my* foxhole!

Now, nearly a year after graduation, I started working with the federal government in Washington, DC.

Vietnam *had* affected me *positively* in the sense that I learned some important life lessons that carried me through my federal government career, several other careers, on into my volunteer jobs with non-profit organizations, and, lastly, now, with my much-loved involvement in the "Dog Show World."

Service in Vietnam *opened the door* for me, as it did for many of our servicemen. Among other things, *I learned* about the importance of *confidentiality* from my time in the military service. *You protect your country, family, friends, and place of work.*

Thanks to my service in Vietnam, I had no problem getting a "Top Secret Clearance." But I was still very socially naïve, shy, quiet, unused to working in a large office environment, and I thought if I just "worked hard" that would be good enough. People picked up on and commented about my overly formal demeanor and speech. That was a *change* from Vietnam! I had worked well and fit right in with the 101st in Vietnam, where we did not have office politics and did not need the fine layering and nuances of social skills. Unlike in Vietnam, my peers were not covering my back as part of a "team," anymore. Competition was everywhere for plum assignments, promotions, time off, performance ratings, and office perks. Anything you said "in confidence" was "fair game" for passing on to the boss! This was a radical change, and a huge adjustment for me to make.

The "real world of work" with three-piece suits with expensive ties was certainly a lot different than Fatigues. I also had social skills to learn and it was a long process. For most of my high school and college years, I was quiet and some would say socially challenged. I hated public speaking or speaking in front of people—even in the classroom just answering questions or making a comment—as I usually blushed, stuttered, and wanted to get the experience over with as quickly as possible. Although my experience at Camp Evans had helped, I still had some formidable obstacles to work on.

I was actually *unprepared* for what I had to do to survive back *"home"* in the United States.

I tell the kids in class, now, that the "real work world" is a lot different than what we just *teach* you in class. You need your body of knowledge, but you also have to be able to fit into the culture of the business or agency where you are working, because there is a definite "social aspect" in work. It is not just "politics," but rather it is making people feel comfortable when you are with them and then being able to obtain what you need to get your job completed!

That means figuring out what *you need to do* to become a part of a small or large group. In one DC agency, later on, it meant gathering for Redskins football games each Sunday in front of the TV, or playing poker with the men until very early Sunday morning. Another agency had their "Happy Hours" on Fridays and soccer games on Mondays on the Mall. If you started missing out on these things, your promotions could be slow or non-existent.

In my work career, I learned about 4-Martini Lunches, Happy Hours, a few borderline out-of-control Christmas parties, and in one agency came across a drinker crowd where folks went to lunch three to four days a week and did not return to the office on time. I had to get out of some of these activities and groups quickly, as I preferred to stay in the office and work. They called me *"different"*…and I was.

At other agencies, sometimes "lunch" was only a half-hour and we spent most of that time waiting for the elevator, or lining up to eat at a fast-food or take-out restaurant. Then we had to stand up and eat and "socialize." I found it all very stressful, a time waster, and expensive. I started taking my own bag-lunch every day, so I could read the newspaper or work while I ate. Some of this did not help my "standing" with my peers. But I had always enjoyed large periods of time on my own, and Vietnam had reinforced and strengthened this.

I remember being at home in Pittsburgh one time worrying about my job. I had the "work ethic" OK, and I used to go into work on *weekends* to stay on top of the paperwork. I had no real training from my supervisor, but the major problem was that *I just did not fit in.* I remember being *angry* while driving my Ford Mustang 351 and traveling 120-miles-an-hour on the Interstate a few miles from my home! My brother had just spent all afternoon tuning-up the car. Before the night was out, I started driving back home to my Mom's place to pack-up and leave for DC overnight. I ended up over-steering the Mustang around a curve going too fast, and I drove across the road, shearing off the right side of the car on a telephone pole. The car was "totaled" but I was unhurt when the car came to a stop among tree branches. I opened the door and fell down 10-feet into a ravine, hurting my knee (which continued to be a minor problem for the next ten years).

"*It is not my time yet,*" I remember thinking, and I *wondered* what *was going* to happen to *me* in the future, if this *anger stuff* didn't stop.

To save face, I blamed the accident on the car, but the insurance company cancelled me immediately and I ended up buying a 4-cylinder car that could barely get up enough speed on a ramp to merge on a main road artery. That was the end of speed for me. That Mustang had "everything" on it, and I really felt sorry for what I had done to the car, *and* to Bernie.

Because I had been a Personnel Clerk in Vietnam, I went into Personnel/Human Resources ("HR," now) with the federal government. At the time, it was pretty much a white-male-dominated profession at the top, but that changed over the next thirty years. I switched jobs a few times and, as I tell the kids in class, sometimes you move up, sometimes you get kicked down, and sometimes you make a sideward move to get out. I did not have a "straight ride to the top" as a Top-of-the Line "GM-15." When we lose a job, we used to look at such things as failures. But we should look at these experiences as "life lessons," and then you have the opportunity to figure out what you need to do to hold a job, and to get that promotion or good performance rating—if you have the drive and you do not give up. Sometimes, you do succeed, but you seldom know why, completely. On the other hand, if you fail, you can analyze what went wrong, work on your shortcomings, and ride with your strengths.

You do have to survive...and I used to think during the ups-and-downs in my federal career: *If I survived Vietnam, I was going to survive anything.*

From Vietnam, I learned to work long hours and I could focus unbelievably well on a project. I was driven, and so I became a *workaholic*. In Washington, DC, New York, San Francisco, or Los Angeles that is probably not such a bad thing, as the pressure to perform and succeed *is everywhere*. I always seemed to be able to "step it up," if the competition was better.

I still had my handicaps but I was always working really hard on my public speaking and getting my voice heard. I often thought that I would never get over the shyness and stumbling when I talked. For many years, I was too quiet and shy in meetings and in workshops. That held me back from moving ahead faster. I see the few shy kids there are in classrooms, now, and I tell them privately and encouragingly, not as a directive…*"If I made it, so can you, too."* There are not too many shy kids anymore, and my major complaint is that everyone *now* wants to talk at the same time!

In my career, I hated meetings until I realized that they were "OK," if I ran them! I remembered how CW2 Evans ran his meetings and I thought "shorter was better," as we had our work to do, just as in Vietnam.

But, sometimes, the social culture of an agency sets the expectation for constant and long meetings. I just wanted to do my work, but as I rose through management, I had to go to more of these meetings. At one point early in my federal career, one of the many bosses I had told me that I would "always be staff and never a line manager." He told me to consider "getting out of the government," as this is what he saw best for me.

He also told me *I could not write well,* and he spent a lot of time going out of his way to prove his point. I did not believe him!

I did find my comfort zone while writing directives, policy and position papers, vacancy announcements, resumes, job descriptions, and evaluations, and felt at one point that, if I understood the subject matter, I would do all right. For comic relief, my one-time jogging buddy on the Mall in Washington, DC probably remembers the creative resumés I did for fun in ten-minutes' time.

Government writing is considered by many to be bland, straight-forward, and without passion. I had never read a legal document, either, that was warm and inviting. I do believe that I wrote more job descriptions and evaluation statements than probably 95% of the government position classifiers, and I took pride in my finished product, which I enjoyed bringing in under deadline. I had learned how to work for hours at a time like this in Vietnam, as I had to produce, or I would get reassigned to the field with a M-16, where the probability of returning in a body bag was significant enough that I did not need to worry about probability estimates, correlation coefficients, and standard deviations, as I was taught at Penn State in business statistics classes.

If I had to do presentations, or have meetings all day that were stressful, then I *needed* my "down time" and time to myself. Some get recharged with solitude, and others need constant stimulation from people and need that social interaction. I preferred accomplishing work and having time for reflection and downtime.

My delight and satisfaction in writing within my government positions helped me to realize that writing was something I really enjoyed. As the years moved on, I did more and more writing at an increasingly sophisticated level, and it became embedded in my spirit— although it was not fulfilled until years afterward during my retirement.

CHAPTER 34

Welcome to "PTSD"...
But, Who *Knew It?*

I remember the evening two guys in Washington, DC approached me in the mid-1990s as I was getting my car from an outdoor parking lot after work and the sun was setting.

It was cold, I was bundled up in my green Burberry topcoat, and the two guys said they "wanted my wallet and all my credit cards."

I said, coldly and without any emotion, "No. Go bother someone else...you do *not* want to mess with *me*."

The guys looked at each other, laughed, and walked away.

The next day as I got my car from the same lot at the end of the day, the new parking lot attendant told me that yesterday's parking lot attendant was robbed, knifed, and died while he was in his heated booth.

Had I a lot of time to think about the request for my wallet in the almost isolated parking lot, I would have given up the wallet, ring, and my watch, too.

What I did, in standing up to the two guys, I knew had to have come from my Army training. If I choose to back down, that is my choice. But sometimes, your instincts take over. I was not *trained* to be a Chaplain's Aide.

Once or twice a year I would overreact in the federal government—especially if there was an injustice to someone else, or if someone made a comment about my lack of hearing. I would get instantly hot in the back of my neck, and overreact. Much later in life, I learned about the *options* we all have to be assertive, passive, or aggressive. You pick and choose, but I was not in a *war zone* anymore, so I should *not* have had so many aggressive responses.

Most times, I was usually as surprised as my target, because I did not know at the time where my aggressive response was coming from.

I generally tried not to put myself in these situations as I knew I was vulnerable because of my time in a war zone and, I really did not want to hurt anyone. I remembered the kid from New York, though, who thought he could keep taking my *Cokes*. Had he connected with his swing at me, I *was* going to defend myself. Now, as for the Boxer, I would just leave him alone.

When thrown into a confusing party-like atmosphere, I continued to be very *nervous* and could not *relax*. Some of this was Vietnam staying with me, but I also have a core personality, too, that *craves order, predictability, and being by myself.* I used to feel guilty, but I had to be true to myself.

Along the way, I picked up running every day as a way to stay *calmer*, and I joined a health club and started to become more aware of my health. I had ended up with fallen arches in my late-20's from running in poorly fitting shoes and began to wear orthotics. The podiatrist I was seeing said I would not be running when I was 40, so I should get used to the idea. *I still run a little at age 68*—so, again, this is an example of my propensity to not always listen to the "experts" who predict what will happen to me, or who say "it cannot be done."

I tell the kids in the classroom, "If you want to do something *badly* enough, you *will* find a way!"

Even though I had a rough beginning in my federal career with delayed and slow promotions and a failure to finish a probationary period, I ended up being a Personnel Officer with one agency, HR and EEO Director with another small and independent agency, and finally HR Director for a sub-agency, from which I retired at age 53 in 2002. I still preferred to eat my lunches by myself most of the time, while reading newspapers.

I have to credit that Vietnam Service with reinforcing in me that I was going to make it, no matter the odds. Very few careers are straight to the top. I probably took a few more hits than most on the way, but I learned from each experience. I am still not sure how I made it, but I never did give up. I did not know how to.

The Army, and Vietnam, made me into a real fighter on the inside.

CHAPTER 35

Married Life and a New Future

I had an unrequited love interest in the late 1970s and spiraled into a long period of anxiety, depression, and self-medication.

The VA, as well as medical/mental health counselors, didn't know much about Post Traumatic Stress Disorder (PTSD) at the time. But from this new, triggering, stressful situation, I soon had my *flashbacks*, and also *panic attacks* in stores and closed rooms.

In one case I remember I was driving down the road in Springfield, Virginia when the whole road appeared to *visually roll up on me!* I stopped driving the car, and started psychological counseling immediately thereafter, which got me straightened out. However, some heavy doses of self-medication delayed the full recovery.

I did get through all this, and learned so much more about myself as a result. I got stronger at work, but went through a foggy period for a while.

I also began to take on a lot of volunteer jobs to fill-in the time. I do believe we should give back, and I have had much to be thankful for, including my education—because of Social Security and GI Bill funding, but I took on way too much!

I had a great federal career, and in one position I got to travel as a nurse recruiter for many years to most of the major cities on the East Coast. Later on, I traveled deep into U.S. coal mines perhaps fourteen times—watching the "open-continuous" (done by machinery by remote control) and "long-wall mining" (approximately two football fields in length) at its best.

**Visiting a Surface Mine near
Beckley, West Virginia.**

I visited a salt mine below Lake Erie that had been closed off before the dinosaurs' period of over 330-million years ago, and a silver mine in Wallace, Idaho. I visited The White House three times for the "Christmas-tree display," saw three U.S. presidents from a brief distance, and visited just about every Memorial, museum, and office building in Washington, DC—including the Capitol, Supreme Court, and Library of Congress. My *Rex* book is now in the Library of Congress.

I have traveled to Warsaw, Paris, London, and Canada and to different West Coast cities for vacation, including about fifteen trips to Hawaii.

I began coaching and then managing Little League baseball teams in Springfield, Virginia. I ended up spending almost *eighteen years* in Little League, Big League, Babe Ruth, or Special Olympics. I coached, managed, kept score, picked up and dropped off the kids, cleaned up the field and limed the bases...and I found that *the more I had to do, the more I enjoyed it.*

I had some strong management and analysis skills which had already started to show up but I did not pay much attention because these were "just" volunteer jobs. This was the best way to practice being in charge of projects, programs, or a club. One year, I received the title of "Senior Minor League President," but we did not have enough kids to field the minimum of four teams! Yet, I was still kept on the Board of Directors. **I even received a personal letter from Danny Murtaugh, Manager of the Pittsburgh Pirates, commending me for my service. He led the Pirates to the "1960 World Series" and to the "1971 World Series," which I had listened to on the radio in Vietnam! He stated:**

"June 6, 1976.... It is a difficult thing for a coach to teach baseball fundamentals and instill good sportsmanship and competitiveness, at the same time insuring that the boys have fun. You have been able to achieve this rare blend and I congratulate you in your accomplishment."

The Pittsburgh Pirates World Series Victory, 1971.

I also became a basketball coach for two or three years in the Northern Virginia Youth League. The highlight was watching Billy King make his first basket (he put the ball in the opposing team's net, after stripping the ball from an opponent at mid-court), and then following him as he made "All American," Duke Athletic Director, and later New York Nets General Manager in 2010. At least we didn't ruin him. We can't claim that we taught him to shoot, either, as he made his mark as a defensive specialist. I used to pick him up in my car and drive him to practice and the games.

I remember when all the "scouts" came out to watch this "new kid," who was just a very young teenager. He was a very coachable and likeable player and ended up being better than the teacher! That is every teacher's or coach's wish!

In the early 1980s I started a long period of playing tennis regularly. I also played competitive duplicate and rubber bridge, and *then* I started horseback riding, including Dressage Eventing with a Belgian Warmblood. Later, I bought my own horse, "Skylark," who was ¾- Clydesdale and ¼ -Thoroughbred. I liked jumping with "Skylark," and she took me over a 4-foot High Jump once and I landed *successfully!* That was my "goal," and I used to take her out myself on a farm that had 200-acres, taking two to three foot high A-frames regularly.

I started in the "Samoyed Dog World" in 1991 with dog shows, dog sledding, sheep herding, and dog clubs. All of this was *good*, as it "balanced" the work world with its challenges and stresses. When something isn't going well, it is advantageous to have "outside activities." I probably went overboard, but the self-medication stopped for a few years, as did the snuff and pipe tobacco habits. I quickly found myself replacing the basketball and softball/baseball clubs with Officer positions in dog clubs.

I still followed my sports teams from Pennsylvania, though, and I remember my two grad school roommates and I flew to the "Rose Bowl" in Anaheim, California in 1995. Michael and Paul were not happy with the seats they had, which did not give them as good a view as they were used to—as they were over-25-year ticket holders in Beaver Stadium. I sat in the end zone as Ki-Jana Carter broke a few tackles on the first Penn State play from scrimmage to score on almost an 80-yard touchdown run! He came down to my end of the stadium. Penn State beat Oregon easily, and I thought about how *lucky* I was to still be *alive* ... sitting in the uncovered end zone with a hat on and enjoying the game.

I thought of Vietnam and how far I had come.

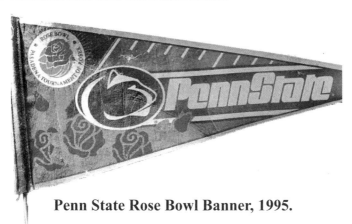

Penn State Rose Bowl Banner, 1995.

I thought of the many others that I had left or were left over there who could not be attending. I had a few tears in my eyes, but kept the sunglasses on and no one knew the difference. I am still not sure how I did all of this, but within two years of owning my first Samoyed, I was Treasurer of one local Samoyed club and then became Treasurer and then quickly Recording Secretary of another.

The *"Point of Light Award,"* 1993, The White House.

I even received one of President Bush Sr.'s *"Point of Light"* pins for volunteer-work, as someone had nominated me from my government job. I still wear the pin proudly on my blue blazer—when I "Steward" (help the Judge) at dog shows.

I remember having to leave a dog show early so I could go to play bridge, and hearing Patty (a breeder from Virginia) remark that I needed to "get my *priorities* in order." For me, though, my *need* was "keeping busy." Within three years, I was Treasurer of the National Samoyed Club for two years and then National President for two more years.

Along the way of being National Treasurer, I met my wife-to-be, Celinda, at a Samoyed Club of America National Dog Show in 1997. She was a well-established breeder/exhibitor, and was working in Hospitality that year.

We were married in 1999.

**Celinda and me heading off to the Reception in style—
led by Steve Loper's team of Samoyed show dogs.**

After the honeymoon, when I returned to my office, I received two promotions in *eight* days and a *third* promotion to "GS-15" six months later! (That is not a record, but it does happen.)

So, now, I was: 1) newly married, 2) the new President of the National Samoyed Club, and 3) a new HR Director! That should be enough for three people to handle! When I got my promotion to GS-15, I wrote my own job description. I should have been able to do it, as I had written thousands over the years—for everyone else.

However, my PTSD issues, which are not as bad as with some Veterans, would show up periodically with the stress, and I needed my quiet time. I had grown used to the daily adrenaline rush which had started with my first Personnel Officer job in 1988, but now it had gotten dangerously stressful at work, and I had a lot of physical symptoms. The stress was there, as it was for most of us in management. I was really good by this point in minimizing the self-medication, which meant that I could be fairly productive although spread thin. But I was spending too much time in meetings at my for-pay job and it was no longer fun. I had a great salary, but an unfulfilling job. I had always thought money was what made most of us happy, but I was finding this not to be so.

I remember where I was on September 11, 2001—watching the TV in a lobby, waiting for a meeting in Rosslyn, Virginia, when first one and then the second plane hit the Twin Towers in New York. I wanted to stay at work (my Vietnam-like bunker) in the unlikely looking Federal Office Building where I worked, instead of going out into the streets and walking or hitch-hiking down to Springfield, Virginia. But by 11:00 a.m., we were all rounded up in the building and sent home, with the office doors locked behind us. I remember walking down "I-95" with thousands of people trying to flee Washington, DC. The rumors had already started about the White House, Capitol, and subway being taken over, or on fire. Vietnam came to mind quickly, with misinformation overload and fabrications. I had been through this before in the War, so I did not feel any panic.

On the way walking toward Springfield, I was picked up by a car filled with Pentagon employees, who confirmed that "something" had hit the Pentagon and part of it was on fire! It only took 90-minutes (instead of 45-minutes) to get home and I surprised Celinda by showing up so quickly.

I talked with her about "getting out of DC as quickly as we could!"

My office moved to another building in Rosslyn, which was a very tall building and I worked on the 19th floor—for about a month. They were not going to keep me much longer than that! I never relaxed in the new office as I do not like to be a "standing target" for anyone. I did *tremble* almost every day in that new office. I had been through that three decades earlier and I did not like the feeling of helplessness. Most of my co-workers had no such problems.

With Brutus in 1971.

With Riley in 2011.

CHAPTER 36

My Second Career in The Dog Show World …
A *Different* Kind of "Dog Tags"

Celinda and I left Virginia for Woodland, Washington on July 3, 2002 as "Independence Day" for me was going to be my first day as a retired federal employee at age…53…on the early out. I had always admired those who took early retirement and here I did it! I did not want to stay longer to get the holiday pay and I wanted out of DC.

We sold our house in Springfield, Virginia quickly and moved to Woodland, Washington to take over a dormant kennel, except for a few Beagles.

Like any marriage we had great times, and like other couples we had some interesting times.

Celinda and me in Hawaii at "The Dole Plantation," Oahu, Hawaii.

Celinda and me with Judge Rudy Munoz, Christie Smith (a Breeding Partner with Celinda), and Seattle— "Best In Show at a Specialty" in 2007.

I guess I should not have been surprised, but I got bored very quickly after a few weeks of unpacking, and I needed a job. The kennel was soon full of dogs as we set up a business, and I started working as a substitute teacher in the state of Washington in Battle Ground, La Center, Kalama, and Green Mountain. I learned "to fish" (no, not really, it just "sounds good" when related to the concept of "retirement"). I cut grass with the John Deere riding-mower and weed-trimmer on five acres, while Celinda took care of showing the dogs. I burned up three transmissions on that first John Deere.

After a lull, the dog clubs started beckoning to me. First, I was Treasurer with The Samoyed Club of America for six or seven years and then President of the local Samoyed Club. All along since 1997, I had stayed on as Treasurer for The Samoyed Club of America Health

and Education Foundation. I was really good on not using the self-medication, but I was *jumpy* at the noises from barking dogs, nosy neighbors, and constant activity. I had no "down time" that I could look forward to, with work and three dog clubs combined to present daily crises.

**Riley, at left with Heather Kelly; Me;
Alan Stevenson, handler, with Ono
(Riley's sire); Christie Smith;
and Celinda, with Mia (Riley's sister).**

I remembered as I was sorting out pictures for this book that there was a moment at the National Cathedral's bookstore, when I was dating Celinda, that I looked at the books and said to her, "If I had it to do over again, *I would have liked to be a writer!*"

Once again, that embedded desire surfaced.

**Celinda and me in front of
the National Cathedral in
Washington, DC.**

CHAPTER 37

Agent Orange Revisited

While in a boat on the Columbia River around 2007, looking for that elusive salmon, my neighbor Bob explained the *"Agent Orange* Registry" and how the VA was providing Vets with free annual physicals—especially if they had been "In-Country." I told Bob I was healthy and did not *need* any "free medical care" from the government, as I had my own insurance. I had been reading about "Vet problems" since I returned in 1972 but always figured I was immune, as it had seemed that "someone" was always watching out for me while I was over there.

But, for some reason, I decided to call up just for information and the call led to my physical within a few weeks. The VA gave me some cholesterol matters to work on, and set me up for a free physical every twelve months.

It was eighteen months later when the VA called *me* and said I should not have *ignored* getting a physical. I was advised if I did not make an appointment within thirty days, I would be deleted from the system and would have to start all over as an outsider or newcomer. I went for my second physical in Vancouver, Washington, and the Family Nurse Practioner (FNP) noticed a *"rise in the PSA"* over the previous period. He arranged for another blood draw very quickly and I was soon set up for a biopsy and ultrasound within thirty days, this time at the Portland, Oregon VA.

It seemed that because of *Agent Orange's* residual impact, Vietnam was just not going to let me forget about my Service time over there!

I made my appointment date and was told by the lab technician that some guys just ignore the appointment for the biopsy and break off contact with the VA and go into denial. I did not do that. My ultrasound scan looked good but the biopsy report in a few days showed that the prostate was cancerous. Celinda and I met with the chief surgeon (who is a world class surgeon also on staff as chief surgeon with Oregon Health and Science University) for options and probabilities of each procedure. We elected the radical prostatectomy as it offered the best long-term survival rate—given my Gleason score and the aggressiveness of the cancer.

While it is true that if a guy lives long enough into his 90's or over 100, he will probably have prostate cancer at an advanced age and surgery usually isn't always the best option. I was 60 and they saw a long life in me still to come. From once viewed as "expendable," the government was now taking care of me!

As was typical of Vietnam Vets, the average age of prostate cancer diagnosis is 60, and we were "showing up" with cancer six to ten years earlier (depending upon the study) than non-Vets. *Agent Orange* was presumed to be the cause.

It does not just show up in the prostate with cancer, as it can work around and through all of the major internal organs.

I had my surgery scheduled for February but an opening in the surgery schedule developed at the Portland VA and I was called in late December by telephone while in Hawaii. At that point, I had worked myself up to 100 push-ups per night, because I was worried about blood clots, blocked heart valves, or a stroke, but they told me I had a strong heart before the surgery and **"not to worry."** My two younger brothers and Dad all had their heart issues, requiring at least multiple stent work or worse but, like my sister, it looked like I had Mom's family heart history and not my Dad's. We do not get to choose which side the dominant genes come from and we do not usually know until we dig around with surgery or have a health problem.

The night before the surgery, I did *101* push-ups—in honor of and remembrance of the *101st* (and also for "good luck")!

I was operated on January 2, 2009. As the cancer had become aggressive, every day was critical to me in *my* mind. If you catch prostate cancer early, you contain it, or it can spread to the lymph nodes and the bone and then you worry about the cancer quickly spreading to your internal organs. We had a few weeks to work with but I did not want to wait until February.

I remember being very *stressed out* before the surgery. I thought I would not survive it as I had made it through my tour in Vietnam. So I told myself if I could survive getting sent over to the jungle 10,000 miles away as a 22-year-old, I would make it this time also! At the time of the surgery, my blood pressure from the stress was extremely high. They brought that down slowly with some drug and then administered the anesthesia. I never felt anything during the surgery as they put me to sleep within seconds and I did very well in the six-hour procedure.

Fear can be paralyzing. I thought I had left this stuff back in Vietnam.

The team of doctors met me after the surgery and told me with my drive and diligence, I was a model patient, and I should make a complete recovery. I thanked the three surgeons who graduated from Cornell, Notre Dame, and USC, respectively, for taking care of me. I never cared for Notre Dame in football since my teenage years but from that day forward, I had a renewed appreciation for Notre Dame graduates.

Aware of the fact *that USC had beaten Penn State in the Rose Bowl the day before my surgery* on January 1, 2009, I thanked the surgeon from USC (who looked like he could have started at middle linebacker) for going to Medical School instead of being a football player for USC, as he would have wrecked his hands playing ball. The world-class prostate cancer surgeon from Cornell performed as lead surgeon with his hands, instead of using the da Vinci robot.

A Catholic chaplain stopped in to visit while I was on my back in the VA bed hooked up with a button to self-administer morphine for the moderate pain I experienced. We talked about Vietnam, and what I was going to do with my *time* after surgery recovery.

Good question—what *was* I supposed to be doing for the rest of my life?

For the first time in my life, someone *asked me* why I had all the for-pay and volunteer work that I was involved in. *Why* did I have to have many things going on at *once?*

And...*what* was I so *afraid* of?

I know, now, that he was "on to something," but at the time I said I was just a "workaholic," like most in Washington, DC that are highly successful, and that I had been like this since I came back from the Service.

He thought that I should think about scaling it back and gave me his Chaplain's card. I have thought since about what he said, a few times over the years, and finally realized, only recently, that I do not have to be like this unless I want to.

I went back home hooked up with a Foley catheter after a two-night stay at the Portland VA. Celinda had a full dog kennel, so on the second morning back home, I was out early working in the kennel helping to provide water for the kennel dogs. Within a few more days I was getting up by myself to take care of the kennel with the Foley catheter hookup fully operational for a good three weeks. I worried a little about the frosting-over of the tubing under a loose fitting bathrobe, as it was early January and the temperature was around the freezing mark. I never did tell the VA that I was doing that kind of stuff. They would *not* have laughed.

Forcing myself to get up and move around early after the surgery was good for me, but there would be no weight lifting for a few months yet and the fogginess from the surgery and morphine was going to be with me nine to twelve months. Although I had barely a scratch from my actual Service in Vietnam, the *Agent Orange* exposure finally presented itself with my cancer, and "got me" *nearly four decades later.* The VA quickly put me on a temporary 100% disability rating in probably record time, but I had some great help from the Vancouver VFW, and from my friend Tam back in DC. She went outside of her SES job description to help.

The Portland, Oregon and Vancouver, Washington VA both took excellent care of me and were aggressive on testing and treatment. I am very fortunate that the Vancouver VA caught my cancer markers early, which led quickly to the radical surgery.

My friend, "B.J.," who fought his own long cancer battle and died in January of 2013, once told me my cancer was coming back, as it had for him. He was not even a doctor, but a highly decorated Airborne Ranger who just *knew*.

He was awarded the highly coveted "Master Blaster" Award, given to those talented and trusted parachutists who have made more than *fifty* jumps!

B.J.'s "Master Blaster" Parachutist Award for over *fifty* Jumps in service to our country.

These are only some of "B.J.'s" Medals. He had over seven tours ("Campaigns"), lasting from six months to one year each. He was a quiet, unassuming "hero," who served his country in full measure.

There are still a good number of us left, but each week brings more obituaries in *The Oregonian* and *The Columbian*, and in hard copy or online digital newspapers across the country of those who served in Vietnam.

Even with my initial cancer surgery and cancer return, *I am glad I served and have never regretted serving as a draftee*. When you are called, you do serve!

But there is no reason to not be informed and try your best to survive—even in a war zone. Now, some of the kids in the classroom don't even know what it means to be drafted. The only draft they have grown up with involves the NFL or the NBA.

The VA took care of me with regular follow-up visits and tests. The VA FNP asked me to consider giving up even the occasional drink, as all this did was slow down the healing from the surgery. Anyone should strive to be completely healed. It was a challenge to work hard with weights, swimming, and running but I wanted a complete recovery. Giving up the snuff years before was tougher for me than not drinking anything. To show that people can come back from cancer and that their life is not over because of cancer, I ran unopposed for the Presidency of The Samoyed Club America. I was not that sharp or even 75% recovered when I accepted the nomination during the summer of 2009 and was banking on continual improvement.

I took a risk and had a plan to get better.

If I did not get better, I was going to have to resign quickly. I just could not accept that I was not going to get better. There were other candidates they could have asked but I thought it was my turn again. If they had only known how weak I still was and that my thinking was not clear yet. After a few months and a few crises, my resolve and mind sharpened and I had a better and more satisfying period of President this time compared to eight to nine years earlier.

The marriage didn't make it, though, as the cancer seemed to be the last stone that was needed to topple the marriage.

We were a mismatch and some now tell me they had bets we would not make it through the first year of marriage. However, Celinda and I parted as friends after thirteen years and have remained friends to the present.

My PTSD instances and the need for quiet, along with other issues, were now coupled with the cancer diagnosis, surgery, and recovery. Celinda said, given that I survived Vietnam and my younger brother Bernie's recent death earlier in 2009 from diabetes and complications, I would survive this, too, as *"I was a survivor."*

I looked around at the five Samoyeds in the house, realized they needed me and I like to think the Samoyed Club of America needed me, too. I did not have a choice, as I had to make it through this, too, and put one foot in front of the other to make it through until I could hit 3rd gear again. From watching the Penguins and Steelers win the Stanley Cup and Super Bowl, respectively, right after surgery in 2009, I was on an up-and-down roller coaster ride all year.

Not self-medicating helped, and you just have to go through the stages. You have no choice. Others had made it, so I could do it, too. I found a wonderful counselor, as I was not going to spend any more time than I had to on grieving.

I learned a lot about myself, but these were tough lessons.

My 101st Cap.

PART FOUR

Celebrate *Life!*

A Pastoral View from one of my Windows.

CHAPTER 38

Now-a-Days

I don't know how I would have acquired the drive to work as I do without my Vietnam Service. I did not have this kind of drive before Vietnam, except in sports. I finished out the year 2010 as Samoyed Club of America President, local Samoyed club President, and Treasurer for The Samoyed Club of America Foundation. Riley won "Best in Show" at the Samoyed National Specialty in 2011 at age 10-and-a-half, beating all 316 Samoyeds entered!

I kept up my regular VA appointments and for almost eighteen to twenty months there was no movement from the Prostate Specific Antigen (PSA) test. This is one of the cancer indicators, but I had no prostate remaining so I should not have had any significant PSA reading. I thought I was home free of cancer and could put that little worry behind me. As with anyone who has ever had cancer, you maybe are never in the clear and always get apprehensive before the next test—whether for breast, ovarian, colon, prostate or any of the other cancers.

Then the PSA started to show up as ".1," then a little later as ".2" and then it went to ".3." The tests were spread out every three months once the rise started. The Internet (Brady Institute) says when the PSA is at ".2," *most* health authorities consider it indicative of the recurrence of prostate cancer. When the PSA hit ".3," then it looked like all the Internet sites viewed that as the biochemical return of prostate cancer.

The VA schedules you for a radiation appointment when you hit ".4." For my May 2013 blood draw, the PSA reversed itself and went down to a ".2." How that happened, we are not sure, except I take 10,000 mg. daily of Super Curcumin (an anti-inflammatory), walk or run daily, swim, exercise, and lift weights, don't take any drugs or drink, and pray. Then the PSA went back up to ".3" with the September 23, 2013 blood draw. We continued to monitor it, and then in November 2014, I began radiation at Oregon Health and Science University.

After thirty-five sessions, the PSA marking went down by ½!!! In May 2015, all of the

cancer had gone. A *bona fide* success.   The VA sees a lot of Vets who come in to the Portland and

Vancouver Medical Centers. Both facilities tell me I am in better shape than almost all the other

Veterans that they see. I had to get in shape for the surgery and stay in shape for the recovery!

All of this helps so I can continue to be a "survivor." As the Portland VA urologist tells me, I

have had a pretty full life, maybe enough for several people!   Outside of cancer containment, I

still do not need medications or drugs for any condition such as for blood pressure, diabetes, or

cholesterol. Statistically, I am unusual in that regard.

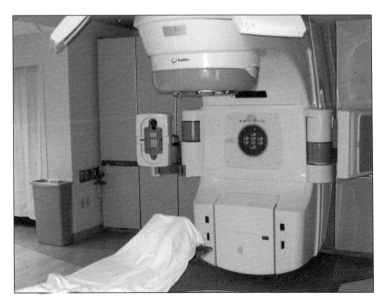

**This is the up-to-date LINAC radiation machine,
and the small bed where I laid as it hovered over me.**

I am also unusual—and grateful—that I have been able to write one book, and now a second! And, with this second book, as with my first, *The Story of Rex of White Way, The Blizzard King,* I have had a small "window of opportunity" for each and I have "jumped" through them. (Rex was "famous" for jumping through open windows when he wanted to get outside for a jaunt, or to meet an appealing female!)

Now-a-days, *Rex* has continued to do well, winning gold and silver medals. I have met other Vietnam Veterans teaching in the southwest Washington public schools. I have not seen another Vietnam Vet teach Kindergarten or preschool but I have subbed there also. Kindergarten requires different skills than at the high school level but some facets remain the same: organization, classroom management, communication, fairness, and you have to like what you are doing or it is not fair to the students.

The VA urologist and I think it will not be the cancer that gets me but the usual things that happen to guys when they get really old.

I should be retired but I enjoy work too much with sub-teaching, therapy work in assisted living places with Riley before he died and currently with Cami, with running the boarding kennel, and I even started volunteering as a football coach in 2015 for La Center High School.

I am continuing as an Author, and maybe I have even found a new career!

I still Steward at dog shows and I serve as Show Chair for the local Samoyed Specialty Dog Show. I have gotten used to saying "No" more recently when asked to volunteer. **But I still want to give back, as I feel that much has been given me.**

I have slowed it down on purpose to keep the stress level low, which should correlate with favorable PSA test results, maybe. I am even getting better anticipating another PSA test on the schedule predetermined by the urologist.

It is not easy, but at some point you have to stop worrying about negative test results and...JUST LIVE!

Specialty Judge Tami Lynch, Me, and Riley.
Courtesy Randy Roberts, Dog Show Photographer,
Leavenworth, WA.

After serving three terms as President (1999–2000, 2001–2002, and 2009–2010),
I am still active in The Samoyed Club of America, and
serve on the Board for the National SCA.
I Steward in my local chapter,
Willamette Valley Samoyed Fanciers Club, and for area shows, and
am also the Treasurer and Show Chair for my local club.

**Me and Faithie hiking for credit in the "Working Samoyed"
Program, with Mt. Hood in the background.
(NOTE: She is wearing a weighted backpack.)**

Rebel with the *Cats* Program.

Honor.

One of the most gratifying projects to work on has been the not-for-profit "Rex of White Way Samoyed Memorial Library and Museum." Donated materials have come in already from several significant sources, most notably the Jim Osborn and Walt Kauzlarich Collections, and from the Madelin Druse Estate, with thanks to her daughter Tania Kaylor for her support and help.

The records, pictures, catalogues, books, magazines, newsletters, and historical Samoyed correspondence have yet to be classified, catalogued, and stored. There are two Annexes at the moment, one in Mt. Shasta, California being coordinated by Celinda Cheskawich, and one in Woodland, Washington being coordinated by me.

The Facebook and Website pages for *The Story of Rex of White Way, The Blizzard King* have had continual updating to reflect the acquisition of new materials, links, awards, or events. Over the next few years, the Library will have a greatly expanded on-line digital presence as well as a permanent physical location.

The Board of Directors are: President, Connie Rudd, Gunnison, Colorado; Treasurer, Barb Barkhaus, CPA, Hartford, Wisconsin; Secretary, Erica Flahaut, Paxton, Illinois; Board Members, Celinda Cheskawich, Mt. Shasta, California, Heather LoProto, Mt. Prospect, Illinois, and Lynda Tusoni, Angels Camp, California. All of them are members of SCA and are established Samoyed breeders.

Books from the Rex of White Way Samoyed Memorial Library and Museum, Mt. Shasta, California Annex.

**Rex of White Way Samoyed Memorial Library and Museum Collection,
Mt. Shasta, California Annex.**

**Some of the book collection in the Rex of White Way
Samoyed Memorial Library and Museum, Woodland, Washington Annex.**

**(Photographs from Mt. Shasta, California Annex by Celinda Cheskawich;
photograph of books from Woodland, Washington Annex by Author.)**

CHAPTER 39

Author's
Concluding Remarks

Even though I worked in Washington, D.C. in the South Interior Building in the late 1980s and 1990s, it took me several years before I could visit the Vietnam Veterans' Memorial, which was across the street (Constitution Avenue) from where I worked. I just could not do it right away.

As I described earlier, when applying for work after graduate school, I kept my Vietnam Service off of my resume for many years. I knew that it was going to hurt me if I was connected to Vietnam. We all knew it.

While working for the federal government in Washington, DC, I heard too many times stories about how the brother or uncle had come back from Vietnam and, "Well, that guy hasn't been *right* since...."

It always made me angry to hear that kind of talk.

Making jest of Vietnam Vets should be repellant to all of us. Vietnam Service certainly provoked disturbing behavior in some, and it is not to be forgotten that even some of the older, established Veterans groups in the U.S. did not want to *accept* Vietnam Veterans as members because of this.

I had to pick my times for viewing any movies on Vietnam. *The Deer Hunter* made me physically sick afterward with the flashbacks. Powerful and riveting, yet fortunately nothing close to the reality of my own personal tour. However, *the fear of death* was always present in Vietnam and the Army training always stressed what could happen in an *instant*. We also knew from Basic Training and Advanced Individual Training (AIT) that if you were captured, the "Hanoi Hilton" was not a five-star resort, which added to the fear of being in the War.

We could not escape reality and some have written that the fear of *"what if"* is worse than what actually happened for most of us. But not all. Over 58,000 of our troops were "Killed in

Action" (KIA), and many, many more returned less than whole, either physically or mentally. Some never came home and are unaccounted for as "Missing in Action" (MIA) or a "Prisoner of War" (POW).

Long after I served, our government came out with a new classification called "Vietnam Era Veteran." This never upset me, as I knew some had enlisted and became fully trained to go to Vietnam to fight for our country, but never served "In-Country." Orders and troop needs fluctuated often during the War so that some never had the chance to serve in Vietnam even though they were ready. As with those in the National Guard, those on the bunker line like me who did not get shot-at too often, are those whom John Milton wrote about in the last line of his poem on *His Blindness*, quoted earlier:

"They also serve who only stand and waite."

In this book I have only written about what I know and what I have experienced, as that is all reality is for me. I was luckier than almost all who served over there.

Each of us who came home had to find a way to deal with Vietnam, and it did not happen right away for me and maybe for most of us.

My brother-in-law, Ron Dallam, who served as a machine gunner with the Marines in South Vietnam, used to watch movies for hours each day, as that is how he coped with the aftermath of his time at war. Ron was a Corporal in the Marines who flew more than twenty combat missions, earning the "Combat Air Crewman Wings with Three Gold Stars."

Ron Dallam's Air Crewman Badge with Three Gold Stars, for twenty Combat Missions.

My sister Colleen always said that, "Ron liked his war movies." He died from leukemia in 1988. Personally, I think that *Agent Orange* should be listed as the "presumptive cause" for his disease. Ron dealt with the War the way *he* knew how, and *I* had my way, too.

You find a way to survive while over there, and you do have to survive when you return to the U.S.

For some, the demons never leave. Others have compromised lives due to physical, mental, or emotional problems.

There were many, many others who served in Vietnam who were just like me, who were equally, if not more, capable of making a difference in government, in volunteer work, as a business manager, or in another field of work. Some never had the chance to make it back, and some came back with too many obstacles to overcome.

Vietnam Service helped turn the switch "On" and it has been there ever since for me. This has often made me feel that I got more out of Vietnam than I gave serving.

> **It was all about duty, honor, sacrifice, and country.**
>
> **We were the very *best* and the *brightest*,**
>
> **who served their country when the Call came.**

As the great humanitarian, Roberto Clemente, is purported to once have told future Hall of Famer, Ernie Banks:

> "When you are on the field, you represent all of your people,
>
> and especially those who did not make it, or fought hard so you could make it.
>
> Stand tall, and run out every hit, and be proud of your heritage."

I am proud to be a Vietnam Veteran.

DEPARTMENT OF THE ARMY

THIS IS TO CERTIFY THAT
THE SECRETARY OF THE ARMY HAS AWARDED

THE ARMY COMMENDATION MEDAL

TO

SPECIALIST FOUR JAMES M. CHESKAWICH,   UNITED STATES ARMY

FOR

EXCEPTIONALLY MERITORIOUS SERVICE
IN THE REPUBLIC OF VIETNAM DURING THE PERIOD JANUARY 71 TO JANUARY 72

GIVEN UNDER MY HAND IN THE CITY OF WASHINGTON
THIS   18TH   DAY OF   DECEMBER   1971

THOMAS M. TARPLEY
Major General, USA
Commanding
101st Airborne Division (Airmobile)

SECRETARY OF THE ARMY

**Original ARCOM
Medal and Citation**

**Recent Commemorative
Vietnam Coins.**

Citation

BY DIRECTION OF

THE SECRETARY OF THE ARMY

The Army Commendation Medal

IS PRESENTED TO

SPECIALIST FOUR JAMES M. CHESKAWICH,   UNITED STATES ARMY

who distinguished himself by exceptionally meritorious achievement
in support of military operations against communist aggression in
the Republic of Vietnam.   During the period

JANUARY 71 TO JANUARY 72

he astutely surmounted extremely adverse conditions to obtain con-
sistently superior results. Through diligence and determination he
invariably accomplished every task with dispatch and efficiency.
His unrelenting loyalty, initiative and perseverance brought him wide
acclaim and inspired others to strive for maximum achievement.
Selflessly working long and arduous hours, he has contributed significantly to the success of the allied effort. His commendable performance was in keeping with the finest traditions of the military
service and reflects distinct credit upon himself and the United
States Army.

**Crowds at The Vietnam Memorial Wall,
Washington, DC.
Photograph by Carl Gernazio.**

"DISCUSSION GUIDE I"
FOR READERS GROUPS
Vietnam 1971—Remembering The 101st Then And Now

"It has taken me nearly *forty-four years* to absorb and process the War to the point where I can finally talk about what I experienced and how the War affected me. Until recently, I wanted to get *as far as away from Vietnam* as possible in my mind. In writing this book, I have found *healing* for myself. It is my hope that *others* will find this, too." —Jim Cheskawich

OPENING DISCUSSION: Remembering Vietnam
- What *three words* would you use to "describe" the Vietnam War?
- Do you have any relatives or friends who lost their lives in Vietnam?
- If yes, what has been their impact or legacy to you?
- What do you think has been the *primary* impact nationally/politically of the Vietnam War upon our country?

VIETNAM WAR STATISTICS
- What do you interpret from the statistics?
- Were you surprised to learn that nearly 61% of those who died were 21 years or younger?

PART ONE: HOW IT STARTED FOR ME
- When (at what age) did you first learn about, or begin to think about, the Vietnam War?
- In general, what is the majority feeling about the War in your community where you grew up?
- If you are in college, or have been in college, is the Vietnam War ever talked about? Is there curiosity about it among your peers?
- Can a Draft be fair?
- Should we still have a Draft, or is the all-volunteer Army better?
- What do you think you would have done with a Draft notice during the Vietnam War?
- Do you believe that everyone should serve two years in service to our country?
- Do you think that you could "make it" through Basic Training?
- If you had to serve, what would you want to be trained as?
- How easy do you think it is to be trained to fight in a war?

- What would you do in the three weeks allotted before going into a war zone?

- What books would you take or want to read in a war zone?

- What would you take with you of personal belongings?

- Do you think that the Vietnam War protesters and music at the time contributed to bringing the War to a close, or did it hinder our involvement?

- Should U.S. Presidents have experience in the military before committing the country to wars?

PART TWO: "IN-COUNTRY" WITH THE 101ST AIRBORNE

- What common issues/problems do you think most soldiers face in a war zone?

- What would be <u>your</u> biggest concerns?

- What would you expect the first week in a war zone to be like?

- What attributes do you have that you think would help you survive?

- How important is "group identification" as a fighting-unit description (e.g., "The Screaming Eagles")?

The Early Days

- What fears would *you* expect to have in a war zone?

- What would you miss most if you went to war for an extended period?

- What do you think soldiers typically do in a war zone for relief from battle fatigue?

- What would appeal to you?

- How much do you want to please your peer group? (Can you say "no," and make a decision and stick with it?)

- If you saw a soldier doing something wrong or illegal, what would you do? Does it depend? What would you tolerate?

- What is your opinion on the use of drugs and booze during the Vietnam War?

- Have you ever written to a soldier in war to let him or her know of your support?

- What would *you* want to hear about from back home if in a war zone?

- At the time of the Vietnam War, should the *Stars and Stripes* have given *all* news, including the dissent and divide over the War in the U.S.? (Today, with the Internet, all news is available to our soldiers.)

On the Watchtower... Under Fire

- How would you feel about setting up napalm charges, or other harmful charges?

- What would you do if someone didn't want to pull their bunker guard duty or do their share of work as a peer?

- Could you fire on someone if you had to in a war?

- Knowing the difference between the color of the tracers from the enemy and from friendly fire, *would you* fire when you thought it was the enemy?

- How do you think you would react to being in the direct line of enemy fire?

- Would you feel better if you were not alone?

- Would you fire if you were alone, 90-feet-high in a Watchtower?

- Do you have any idea how you would feel as a "survivor" of enemy fire?

- What impact do you think it would have on your life and thinking for your future, having experienced being "under fire"?

"R & R" In Sydney, Australia; Autumn Comes to Phu Bai; Bob Hope Brings Hope to the Holidays

- What is the value of R&R?

- How important are breaks or vacations in your own life?

- What activities would you like to do if you could take a week off?

- What are your options if confronted with a bully (i.e., passive, assertive, or aggressive)? And where did you learn this?

- Can you walk away if that is your best option in a bad situation?

- Who are your heroes and role models? Do they help you in sorting out what to do? How?

- Holidays are not always joyous occasions. What do you think of Bob Hope and other sports and media personalities who have visited soldiers in a war zone?

- How many can you name, going back to our earlier U.S. wars?

- How many can you name during the recent Afghanistan and Iraq wars?

Goodbye, Vietnam! *The Kid Is Coming Home*

- How long do you think it took most of us in Vietnam to show the effects of being in a war zone?

- How long do you think it would take you?

- What effects from a war do you think you would "carry home" with you?

- As a Group, read aloud, line-by-line, *The Kid Is Coming Home.* What moves you the most?

- Which items do you think most accurate for Vietnam Vets returning home?

- Which items do you think most accurately describe returning Veterans today from Afghanistan and Iraq?

- Do you have any suggestions for what we could be doing to help them transition?

PART THREE: HOMECOMING

Home Again; Post-War College Daze; Working for the Feds

- Why do you think that there was not universal support and appreciation for our returning troops from Vietnam?

- How would you feel if you served in Vietnam and received the same "welcome" as most of the Vets?

- Why do you think that the returning Vietnam Vets were treated so badly?

Welcome to "PTSD" ... But Who *Knew* It?

- How long do you think it could take to process through a war experience?

- What other names did we use for combat Vets of previous wars, i.e., "shell shock" and "battle fatigue?"

- IF you know of anyone who has served in the Vietnam War, or any other war, have you noticed an effect to the point where behavior is "observable" to others?

- Do you know of any resources available that you could suggest to help someone?

- Should PTSD be called a "Disease?" (e.g., President George W. Bush believes that *It* should not, and other organizations agree.)

Married Life and A New Future;

My Second Career—In the Dog Show World ... A *Different* Kind of Dog Tags

- What do you think of Government employees?

- Would you encourage someone to work for the Government?

- What do you think is different about working in the military and working as a civilian in the Government, or working in a Fortune 500 Company?

- What skills do you think soldiers learn in the Service that are readily adaptable to civilian jobs?

- Are occupations today becoming more stressful and hard to wind down from? Do you know where to suggest to get help?

- How important is volunteer work, and helping others?

- Would you like to win a *"Point of Light Award"*? Or, do you know anyone who has?

Married … Well, Not So Fast … *Agent Orange,* **The Gift that Keeps on Giving (from Chapter 28);** *Agent Orange* **Revisited (Chapter 37); Undergoing Cancer Surgery and Radiation**

- Do you think a country should easily use similar chemicals to defoliate today?
- Is *"All is fair in war"* still applicable today?
- When do you think our country as a whole was first aware that Vietnam Vets were showing up with cancer-related problems, and dying early?
- Besides excellent medical treatment, what do you think are the keys to living with cancer?

PART FOUR: CELEBRATE *LIFE!*

Now-a-Days

- What are the factors that contribute to a happy quality of life?
- How important is it to "follow your passion," and when should you begin?
- Are you, or someone you know, involved in the "Dog Show World?"

Author's Concluding Remarks

- Why do you think that most people, even today, have a negative reaction at the mention of the word "Vietnam"?
- Do you think that the U.S. could have won the War at some point?
- What do you think caused us to lose? (i.e., many soldiers believe that we were "not meant to win" because of the risks of a World War with China and Russia becoming involved).
- For those who fought in the Vietnam War, how do you think they could be acknowledged favorably today?
- What did you learn from reading *"Vietnam 1971—Remembering The 101st … Then And Now"?*
- What "feeling" did you have when you closed the book?
- IF you could say something to a Vietnam Veteran, what would it be?

EPILOGUE

"Traveling Vietnam Memorial Wall"
"Brothers … you will go to THE Wall soon …" by Michael S. Viehman

- Do you ever plan on visiting The Vietnam Memorial Wall, or have you visited it?
- IF you plan on visiting, why do you want to do so?
- IF you have visited, what was your reaction?

- As a Group, read aloud line-by-line from "Traveling Vietnam Memorial Wall." What part moves you the most?

- Are you inspired to any sort of action? If so, what in particular?

Young troops in Da Nang being entertained by equally young Vietnamese singers and musicians.

"DISCUSSION GUIDE II"
FOR VIETNAM VETERANS READERS AND GROUPS
(And for Reflections by Individual Veterans)
Vietnam 1971—Remembering The 101ˢᵗ ... Then And Now

"It has taken me nearly *forty-four years* to absorb and process the War to the point where I can finally talk about what I experienced and how the War affected me. Until recently, I wanted to get *as far as away from Vietnam* as possible in my mind. In writing this book, I have found *healing* for myself. It is my hope that *others* will find this, too." —Jim Cheskawich

OPENING DISCUSSION: Remembering Vietnam

- When did you serve in Vietnam? Where did you serve? What branch of the Service did you belong to? What was your Rank when you entered? What was your Rank when you ended? Were you drafted or did you enlist?

- What *three words* would you use to describe your experience?

- When you arrived in Vietnam, what were your feelings about the War we were fighting?

- Since returning to the U.S., have these feelings changed? IF so, how?

- What do you think has been the *primary* impact nationally/politically of the Vietnam War upon our country?

"IN-COUNTRY"

- Did you lose any buddies to the War while you were there, or before or after you served? Please share, if you feel able to do so.

- IF you feel comfortable doing so, please share one happy memory and one sad, or enduring, memory.

- Is there anything that you have been *holding on to* from that time that you would finally like to *let go* of? Please reflect upon it, and share, if you would like.

- Did you experience any enemy fire? Did you experience any fighting? Any killing?

- What impact has being in the Vietnam War had upon your life and thinking?

R & R

- Where did you go for R&R?

- IF it was more than one place, please describe the scenery and people, and how you felt being there.

- What it was like to be able to "see and experience" another country or countries?

"BOB HOPE" AND OTHER VISITING PERFORMERS

- While you were in Vietnam, did you have the opportunity to see a "Bob Hope" Tour, or other visiting performers and/or celebrities?

- If so, who were they and what was your reaction?

"THE KID IS COMING HOME"

- Reading through line-by-line, either silently or aloud, how accurate is this document in describing *your* feelings about returning home to the U.S.?

HOMECOMING

- What was your "Welcome Back!" experience? Were you warmly welcomed at the airport? In your community? Elsewhere? By family and friends?

- Why do you think there was not universal support and appreciation for our returning troops from Vietnam?

- Do you think that the Vietnam War protesters and music at the time contributed to bringing the War to a close, or did it hinder our involvement?

- Did you attend "Woodstock?"

- Who were your favorite musical performers at the time of the War?

- Did any particular song, or musical performer, or group *help you* during your transition from the War to life back in the USA?

WELCOME TO "PTSD" ... But Who *Knew It*?

- Upon returning home, did you experience any PTSD?

- Do you know, or have you worked with or been associated with, anyone who has?

- Do you have any current, residual PTSD?

- Do you know the resources available to help you or someone you know?

- Do you think that PTSD should be called a "Disease?" (e.g., President George W. Bush believes that *It* should not, and other organizations agree)

Agent Orange, THE GIFT THAT KEEPS ON GIVING

- Do you know if you were exposed to *Agent Orange?* IF so, where and how, and for how long?

- Do you know anyone who was exposed?

- Do you think a country should easily use similar chemicals to defoliate today?

- Is *"All is fair in war ..."* still applicable today?

- When do you think our country as a whole was first aware that Vietnam Vets were showing up with cancer-related problems, and dying early?

- Are you, or someone you know, currently undergoing treatment for *Agent Orange* exposure?

- Besides excellent medical treatment, what do you think are the keys to living with cancer, or to encouraging someone who is living with cancer?

PART FOUR: CELEBRATE *LIFE*!

Now-a-Days

- What are the factors that contribute to a happy quality of life for you?

- Are you living them, or do you think that you can *now* allow those factors to *bloom* and be *enjoyed?*

- How important is it to "follow your passion?" Are you doing so, or do you think that you can now begin to do so?

- Are you, or someone you know, involved in the "Dog Show World?"

- Do you have, or do you know anyone who does have, "dog books" or other memorabilia or items that could be donated to "The Rex of White Way Samoyed Memorial Library and Museum?"

Author's Concluding Remarks

- What did you learn from reading *Vietnam 1971—Remembering The 101st ...Then And Now?*

- What "feeling" did you have when you closed the book?

- Should we still have a Draft, or is the all-volunteer Army better?

- Do you believe that all young Americans should serve two years in service to our country?

- Should U.S. Presidents have experience in the military before committing the country to wars?

- Is there any way that you think you and your fellow Vietnam War survivors could be *honored* by our country and communities? Please describe.

EPILOGUE

"Traveling Vietnam Memorial Wall"

**"Brothers …you will go to THE Wall soon ..." from Poem "Visit to the Vietnam Wall"
by Michael S. Viehman**

- Have you visited The Vietnam Memorial Wall? What was your reaction? (IF you have not visited The Vietnam Memorial Wall, do you intend to do so in the future?)

- Reading silently, or aloud, from the Epilogue by Michael S. Viehman, what moves you the most?

- Are you inspired to any type of action?

- If you could say something to a fellow Vietnam War Veteran, what would it be?

As I stated in my book, "I am proud to be a Vietnam Veteran."

I hope that you feel that way, too.

Thank you for your service to our country.

Vietnam Service Medal.

Vietnam War Veteran's Cap.

IN MEMORIAM

**Sculpture by Glenna Goodacre,
near The Vietnam Memorial Wall,
Washington, DC.
Photograph by Carl Gernazio.**

STATISTICS

Vietnam War Deaths by:

RACE

SERVICE BRANCH

SERVICE COMPONENT

AGE

Stated Race	Casualties
Native American	226
Caucasian	50,190
Malayan	252
Mongolian	116
Negro	7,264
Unknown	215
Totals	58,263

STATISTICS

SERVICE BRANCH

SERVICE COMPONENT

Service Branch	Casualties
Air Force	2,654
Army	38,209
Coast Guard	7
Marine Corps	14,838
Navy	2,555
Totals	58,263

Component	Casualties
Military Reserves	5,760
National Guard	97
Regular Military	34,545
Drafted	17,672
Unknown	189
Totals	58,263

STATISTICS

BY AGE

(See also P. 22.)

Age	Casualties
17	12
18	3,103
19	8,283
20	14,095
21	9,705
22	4,798
23	3,495
24	2,650
25	2,018
26	1,414
27	917
28	768
29	710
30-39	4,927
40-49	1,156
50-59	121
60-62	4
Unknown	17
Totals	58,263

**Photographs by Celinda Cheskawich,
Spring 2014, from "Traveling Vietnam Memorial Wall"
(built by John Devitt, Norris Shears, Gerry Hauer,
and other Vietnam War Veteran volunteers). As noted previously,
*61.2% who died in the War were 21 years old or younger.***

"Gone, but not forgotten."

In reflecting upon these statistics, I always come around to wondering that if we had *blown North Vietnam off the map and killed all the Communist sympathizers in South Vietnam* (if we could have rounded up everyone), perhaps we could have won the War right away and not been involved over there for so long. But the "fear" among our leaders at the time was that, probably, Russia and China would have quickly gotten involved. So we could not go "all out" to bomb the enemy, as that would have ended in a nuclear war!

It was a high stakes chess game with the "game board" of the world at risk.

However, I think we knew, more and more, as individual soldiers came home, that we were *not* going to *win* it—particularly the last few years at the end before we finally *"pulled out."*

After reviewing some of the available literature about the Vietnam War, I am surprised that we *now know* as much as we do about our troop and enemy movements, about the *covert wars* in Laos and Cambodia, and the simultaneous events going on in the world. One of the teachers I sometimes substitute for, Ms. Shawn Link, even has a "rolled map" in her high school classroom. I pulled it down and used it in September 2013 to show the major battles and how the U.S. forces moved into Laos and Cambodia (shown on her map with large purple arrows!) close to the "Ho Chi Minh Trail." We soldiers and Veterans were *supposed* to keep all of that *secret* from the American people and the world in the 1970s.

I am also still struck by the fact that President Lyndon Baines Johnson (August 27, 1908–January 22, 1973) died very soon, *at age 64,* after leaving the White House. The stress of the War had to have worn him down, as well as the daily taunt, *"Hey, Hey, LBJ! How many kids did you kill today?"*

I just turned 65 a month after starting to write these memoirs. So it would appear the War took the President way too early and that he also was a "casualty" of it. Johnson's Secretary of State during the War, Dean Rusk, of whom it was said that he worked 16-hour days for nearly eight years, also had to have been physically affected by the War.

Many times in recent high school classes I have discussed concepts and lessons learned from two documentaries: *The Unknown Known* by Erroll Morris about former U.S. Secretary of Defense Donald Rumsfeld and *The Fog of War* also by Erroll Morris about former U.S. Secretary of Defense Robert McNamara. I have also discussed McNamara's book, *In Retrospect.*

After the War, my personal story is probably more of a success story than most, but still I had, and I still have, my issues. Many who served in Vietnam became very successful businessmen, working in a trade or craft, teaching, serving in Congress, or working for the federal government. Still, no Vietnam Veteran has made it to the White House as U.S. President although three (Al Gore, John Kerry, and John McCain) ran for the office and were defeated. It does not matter whether Republican or Democrat. As President Dwight D. Eisenhower said in a speech in 1946: *"I hate war as only a soldier who has lived it can...."*

I do think that serving in the Armed Forces should be a requirement for getting elected to the job of President. Maybe we wouldn't be in so many wars.

MAP OF THE HO CHI MINH TRAIL

Ho Chi Minh (1890–1969) was the Communist revolutionary leader of North Vietnam until he stepped down in the mid-1960's. He served as an inspiration to the Communist fighters during the Vietnam War who shared his vision of a united Vietnam. The Ho Chi Minh Trail was a series of trails used by the North Vietnamese to provide troops and supplies to the War in South Vietnam. The beginnings of the Trail are in the Nape Pass area. Parts of the Trail ran through Laos and Cambodia to hide activities from the U.S. Otherwise, the shorter path was to just cross the DMZ into South Vietnam. *Agent Orange* was used by the U.S. to defoliate the vegetation to be better able to see Viet Cong activity along the Trail for American airplane bombing.

Original Map by Brad Johnson.

APPENDIX 1
BRIEF CHRONOLOGY
OF THE VIETNAM WAR

May 8, 1954 Dien Bien Phu fortress fell, marking the end of French colonialism in Vietnam. The U.S., under President Dwight Eisenhower, thereafter began supporting the South Vietnamese government with military and civilian advisors.

December 1960 At this point, there were approximately 980 U.S. advisors in Vietnam. Agroville/Strategic Hamlet programs represented U.S. initiatives.

January 1961 John F. Kennedy began office as our nation's 35th President.

December 14, 1961 President Kennedy pledged support for South Vietnamese independence.

February 1962 Creation of MACV-Military Assistance Command, Vietnam.

1962–1971 "Operation Ranch Hand" sprays almost 12 million gallons of herbicides across Vietnam. *"Agent Orange"* became the most well-known of the herbicides.

January 1963 Battle of Ap Bac which was a test case for using helicopters, armored vehicles, and various tactics in Vietnam. This battle foreshadowed future problems and failures for ARVN and the U.S. The credibility gap involving body counts and kill ratios began with this battle.

November 22, 1963 Assassination of U.S. President John F. Kennedy in Dallas, Texas in a motorcade.

November 22, 1963 Lyndon Baines Johnson becomes 36th U.S. President.

December 1963 Approximately 16,000 U.S. advisors in Vietnam.

August 2–7, 1964 "Gulf of Tonkin" incident involving *USS Maddox* destroyer and
Congressional resolution passed increasing involvement in Vietnam.

February 24, 1965 Regular bombing of North Vietnam began.

March 6, 1965 First U.S. combat ground-forces (Marines) arrive at Da Nang in the undeclared
"War."

August 1965 First major ground forces introduced in "Operation Starlite" as the Marines
stationed at Chu Lai defeated the Viet Cong.

January-March 1968 "Tet Offensive" by the North aimed to cause insurrection in the South.

January-March 1968 "Hue Massacre" at the former Imperial capital of Vietnam where 3,000
residents of Hue were massacred by the NVA/VC and buried in a mass grave in the jungle
outside the city. After a twenty-five day battle, elements of the U.S. 1st Cavalry and 101st
Airborne Division, 1st and 5th Marine Regiments, and numerous ARVN units finally
forced the NVA/VC out of Hue.

January-April 1968 North Vietnamese Army siege of Khe Sanh.

February 27, 1968 Upon Walter Cronkite's return from Vietnam, in an editorial on Vietnam
on his nightly television news program, he called for negotiations to end the War, "not
as victors, but as an honorable people who lived up to their pledge to defend democracy,
and did the best they could." It was claimed by some later that President Lyndon Johnson
said, "If I've lost Cronkite, I've lost Middle America."

March 16, 1968 "My Lai Massacre" by U.S. soldiers against civilians created scandal and
fueled U.S. disaffection with the War.

January 1969 Richard M. Nixon becomes 37th U.S. President.

April 1969 U.S. Forces peaked at 543,400.

May 1969 "Battle of Hamburger Hill" (Ap Bia Mountain) The hill was *abandoned* by the U.S. and ARVN forces *after having won the fight.* The NVA forces returned later unchallenged! This created a powerful negative reaction on the home front because it appeared that our men died in vain.

June 1969–January 1973 U.S. progressively withdraws forces from War and implements "Vietnamization."

September 3, 1969 Ho Chi Minh dies.

May 4, 1970 Kent State University students killed during ant-War demonstration.

June 24, 1970 Repeal of the "Gulf of Tonkin Resolution."

March-October 1972 North Vietnamese "Eastertide Offensive" rebuffed, and U.S. responded with aerial bombings in May and December.

July 1972 Actress Jane Fonda visits Hanoi, North Vietnam generating hatred and much controversy for "visiting" the enemy.

January 27, 1973 "Paris Peace Accords" and U.S. withdrawal after cease-fire.

April 30, 1975 Saigon falls to the NVA/VC, which results in a unified Vietnam under Communist rule. "Operation Frequent Wind" was named for the U.S. helicopter airlift/ pull-out of South Vietnamese from the about to be overrun capital. Saigon subsequently renamed Ho Chi Minh City.

SOURCES: *The Vietnam War for Dummies; The World Almanac and Book of Facts 2012; Wikepedia* on Vietnam War, Walter Cronkite, Fall of Saigon and Jane Fonda.

APPENDIX 2

TERMS, PHRASES, PRODUCTS, ETC. FROM THE 1960s

For those who do not remember those times, or were not even born then, here are some explanations of terms, phrases, products, etc. from the time of this book.

ARVN Army of the Republic of Vietnam (South Vietnam fighting forces allied with U.S. forces).

Blue Book Light-blue-colored booklets used for written examinations in college.

Charlie Used as a collective name for the Viet Cong and the North Vietnamese Army during the Vietnam War.

DMZ "Demilitarized Zone," which is a buffer area (i.e., no fighting to take place there), five miles wide determined by the Geneva Convention, which temporarily divided Vietnam into North Vietnam and South Vietnam.

NVA North Vietnamese Army, officially the Vietnam People's Army, the primary military force of North Vietnam, promoting Communism.

PTSD Post Traumatic Stress Disorder which is a behavioral response to witnessing or experiencing an event or events.

Tang A fruit-flavored drink which may have originally been orange-flavored but also could be in grape or tea flavors. Sold in powdered or ready to drink form and was used in the U.S. manned space flight program, which enhanced its popularity.

VC Viet Cong, a Communist guerilla military force of the South Vietnam Army, commonly know as the "People's Liberation Front" or the "People's Liberation Armed Forces" (PLAF), that was supported by North Vietnam.

Woodstock Music Festival An open air music festival on a dairy farm in Woodstock, New York from August 15-18, 1969 featuring prominent, eclectic, and emerging artists and groups.

SOURCES: *Merriam Webster's Collegiate Dictionary* for Blue Book, Charlie, Tang, VC; *Wikepedia* on Woodstock, VC, Tang: *The Vietnam War for Dummies* for ARVN, DMZ and NVA.

APPENDIX 3

LIST OF "U.S. ARMY RANKS"

Rank: Generals

General George Washington, General of the Armies

General John J. Pershing, General of the Armies (World War I, 5-Star General)

General Dwight D. Eisenhower, General of the Army, Supreme Commander of Allied Forces in Europe, Chairman of the U.S. Joint Chiefs of Staff, Supreme Commander of NATO (World War II-Korean War, 1941-1952, 5-Star General)

General Douglas MacArthur, General of the Army, Supreme Commander of Allied Forces, Southwest Pacific (World War II-Korean War, 1944-1951, 5-Star General)

General William Westmoreland, Commander of U.S. Military Assistance Command Vietnam, (MACV), (Vietnam War, 1964-1968, 4-Star General)

Lt. General (3-Star)

Major General (2-Star)

Brigadier General (1-Star)

Colonel ("Full Bird"), a Silver Eagle Insignia

Lt. Colonel

Major

Captain

First Lieutenant

Second Lieutenant

Warrant Officers (Holds rank by virtue of a "Warrant" approved by the Secretary of the Army; primarily technical experts and specialists.) Grade 5, Grade 4, Grade 3, Grade 2, Grade 1

Non-Commissioned Officers (a subordinate officer appointed from among Enlisted personnel)

Sergeant Major of the Army (E-9)

Command Sergeant Major (E-9)

Sergeant Major (E-9)

First Sergeant (E-8)

Master Sergeant (E-8)

Sergeant First Class (E-7)

Staff Sergeant (E-6)

Sergeant (E-5)

Corporal (E-4)

Specialists (an Enlisted rank equivalent to Corporal, E-4, with subject matter expertise. Higher Specialist Grades above E-4 were discontinued. My promotion in Vietnam would have been to Spec 5, E-5, but it has been fazed out.)

Specialist (E-4)

Other Enlisted

Private First Class (E-3)

Private (E-2)

Private (E-1)

SOURCE: *The World Almanac and Book of Facts*, 2012, World Almanac Books, 132 West 31st Street, New York, New York 10001. Printed and Bound by RR Donnelly, Crawfordsville, IN, p. 139.

APPENDIX 4

DEFINITIONS: MILITARY TERMS AND U.S. ARMY UNITS

Army Headquarters, and two or more Corps with operational and support responsibilities under a General.

Corps Two or more Divisions with Corps troops under a Lieutenant General.

Division Headquarters, and three Brigades with Artillery, Combat Support, and Combat Service Support units under a Major General.

Brigade Headquarters, and two-five Battalions under a Colonel.

Battalion Headquarters, and four-six Companies under a Lieutenant Colonel.

Company Headquarters Section and three-five Platoons under a Captain.

Platoon In Infantry, usually two-four Squads under a Lieutenant.

Infantry Foot-soldiers trained to fight.

Squad In Infantry, usually eight-sixteen Enlisted Personnel under a Staff Sergeant.

SOURCE: *The World Almanac and Book of Facts,* 2012, World Almanac Books, 132 West 31st Street, New York, New York 10001. Printed and Bound by RR Donnelly, Crawfordsville, IN, p. 131.

Credits
Photography, Illustrations, and Artwork

[AUTHOR'S NOTE: All of the below are used by permission unless otherwise noted.]

PAGE NO.	ITEM	CREDIT
Front Cover and 1	Hueys in Combat	"Hueys on a Combat Air Assault," by *Randy Parmley* (Charlie Company, C/2/506th, c1970–71), www.company-c-2nd-bn-506th-inf.com.
Front Cover and 1	The Vietnam Memorial Wall	"The Vietnam Memorial Wall," Photograph by *Tamara Somerville*, 2013.
Front Flap	Jim Cheskawich, Fort Dix, 1970.	Author's Private Collection.
Back Flap	Jim Cheskawich and Cami.	Photograph by Joan Luna. Author's Private Collection.
Page I	American Flag	From *Safeway* Store in Woodland, WA. Author's Private Collection.
Page II	Cemetery	Ft. Vancouver, WA Veterans Memorial Cemetery. Author's Private Collection.
Page III	Near Hue or Da Nang on Cattle Truck	Author's Private Collection.
Page V	"Fire in the Hole" Near Phu Bai	Author's Private Collection.
Page VIII	Author With a Screaming Eagle That Has Landed	Author's Private Collection.
2	Phu Bai, South Vietnam, 1971	Author's Private Collection.
3	Author at Camp Campbell, 1971	Author's Private Collection.
Dedication 6	*"Sons of...."*	With deepest appreciation to *Judy Collins*, her team of Erin Bockman and Katherine DePaul at rockymountainproductionsinc.com and Troy Schreck on behalf of Alfred Publishing Company for permission to use the lyrics of "Sons of" by Brel, Jouannest, Blau, Shuman, Editions Pouchenel S.P.R.L., and Unichappell Music, Inc.
Dedication 6	Judy Collins in Concert	With appreciation to The Image Works, NY. ETPM0272986. Copyrighted picture used with permission and thanks to Lorraine Goonan.
7	Larry Sindelar, B.J. Moses, Dennis Lorenzini, Ron Dallam	Courtesy Mrs. Larry Sindelar; Courtesy Mrs. Sakura Moses; Courtesy The Elizabeth-Forward High School Yearbook, Permission by Elizabeth-Forward High School District. Courtesy Mrs. Colleen Dallam
7–8	Author's Love Beads	Author's Private Collection. Photograph by Minette Siegel.

PAGE NO.	ITEM	CREDIT
8	Vietnam Campaign Medal	Author's Private Collection, from Medals of America Company.
9	"A Beacon Standing for Peace"	Author's Private Collection.
10	Scenes In or Near Phu Bai 1971	Author's Private Collection.
13	Author's Airborne Patch	Author's Private Collection. Photograph by Minette Siegel.
16-17	Vietnam Montage	Annie Reid, Suffield, Connecticut, Original Art, "Doves, Peace, Love, and Non-Violence." Colorization by Desta Garrett. Veterans of Foreign Wars, Robert Widener, Art Director, *VFW Magazine* for the photograph, "Soldiers with the 173rd Airborne Brigade, serving in Vietnam as the first U.S. Army "Ground Combat Unit."
16-17	Vietnam Montage	Caskets of U.S. Servicemen killed in an explosion in Vietnam, being unloaded at Travis Air Force Base in California on May 28, 1965. "Creative Commons" 4.0 CC. License Suite, Public Domain Photograph, originally by *Harry Groom,* for *Newsweek Magazine.* The "Daisy" Photograph, Author's Private Collection. (Daisy from an arrangement purchased from the *Safeway* market in Woodland, Washington by the author.)
21	"Memorial in the Field"	Courtesy of Randy Parmley.
22	Casualties of The Vietnam War	Photograph by Celinda Cheskawich, Spring 2014, from "Traveling Vietnam Memorial Wall (built by John Devitt, Norris Shears, Gerry Hauer, and other Vietnam Veterans volunteers).
24	Portrait of Author, Fort Dix Basic Training, Aug–Oct 1970, age 22	Author's Private Collection.
25	Young troops in Da Nang being entertained by equally young Vietnamese singers and musicians	Author's Private Collection.
26	Stained Glass, The Polish Falcon	Author's Private Collection.
27	Cyrillic Birth Certificate	Author's Private Collection. Scan by Minette Siegel.
28	Author's Godmother, Aunt Leona	Author's Private Collection. Scan by Minette Siegel.
29	Author's Father, Joseph Cheskawich	Author's Private Collection. Scan by Minette Siegel.
29	Penn State "Nittany Lion"	Permission of Penn State University, Maureen E. Riddel, Director, Trademark Licensing.
31	Coach Gene Wettstone	Permission of Penn State University, Maureen E. Riddel, Director, Trademark Licensing.
32	TET Offensive	Author's Private Collection. "101st History of the Screaming Eagles Brochure"; Permission granted by 101st Airborne Division, Fort Campbell, Kentucky.

Page No.	Item	Credit
33	The late Muhammad Ali and Sonny Liston Fight	With deep appreciation to the late Muhammad Ali and his staff.
34	"8" Ball and "2" Ball	Courtesy of the Merwin Tap Tavern, Woodland, WA. Photograph by Author.
35	Portrait of Janis Joplin	With deepest gratitude to Photographer Baron Wolman.
36	Portrait of Jimi Hendrix	With deepest gratitude to Photographer Baron Wolman.
38	Dennis Lorenzini Medals	Permission from Jim Schueckler, Founder and President www.virtualwall.org, Ltd., "The Virtual Wall."
39	The Combat Infantryman Badge	Author's Private Collection, from Medals of America Company. Scan by Desta Garrett.
40	Order to Report for Physical	Author's Private Collection. Scan by Minette Siegel.
44	Photograph of Frank Champ	Author's Private Collection.
46	Issuance of M-16 Weapon	Author's collection. Photograph by Minette Siegel.
47	Fort Ord Brochure Cover	Author's Private Collection.
48	Army-Air Force Exchange Service Top 50 Pops.	Author's Private Collection. Design with arrows by Desta Garrett. Scan by Minette Siegel
50	Photograph of Andy Sedlak	Author's Private Collection.
51	Postcard from Frank Champ	Author's collection. Photograph by Minette Siegel.
53	Author's Family Photo	Author's collection. Scan by Minette Siegel.
55	Double Wamo Supersurvey	Author's Private Collection. Permission from General Counsel Ron Davenport, Jr. of Sheridan Broadcasting Company. Scan by Minette Siegel.
56	Terry Bradshaw Football Card	"Topps 1972 Terry Bradshaw Card." Used by courtesy of the Topps Company, Inc., New York, New York. For more information about the Topps Company, see their website at www.topps.com
57	View of South Vietnam from Airliner Window	Author's Private Collection.
58	"101st History of the Screaming Eagles Brochure" Cover	Author's Private Collection. Permission granted by 101st Airborne Division, Fort Campbell, Kentucky.
61	Author in front of Helicopter	Author's Private Collection.
63	Camp Campbell	Author's Private Collection. Photo restoration by Desta Garrett.
63	Cattle Car (truck behind Author's)	Author's Private Collection. Photo restoration by Desta Garrett.
65	"Operation Hawthorne"	Author's Private Collection. Permission granted by 101st Airborne Division, Fort Campbell, Kentucky.
68	Two fellow Army buddies	Author's Private Collection. Photo restoration by Desta Garrett.

Page No.	Item	Credit
69	Three members of Personnel Unit	Author's Private Collection. Scan by Minette Siegel.
70	Letter from Frank Champ	Author's Private Collection. Scan by Minette Siegel.
71	Envelopes from Frank Champ and Andrew Sedlak	Author's Private Collection. Scans by Minette Siegel
72	Letter from Andrew Sedlak	Author's Private Collection. Scan by Minette Siegel.
73	Phu Bai Administration Building	Author's Private Collection.
74	Photograph of Chinook Helicopter	Courtesy of Randy Parmley.
76	Missalette and Rosary	Author's Private Collection. Photograph by Minette Siegel.
77	Dog Tags	Author's Private Collection. Photograph by Minette Siegel.
77	Military Payment Certificates	Author's Private Collection.
78	Mickey Mantle, "The Mick" Baseball Card	Author's Private Collection. Permission by Tracy Hackler, Panini-America.
79	*Stars and Stripes*	Courtesy of *Stars and Stripes*. © 1971, 2016 *Stars and Stripes*, All Rights Reserved. Thanks to Catharine Giordano.
81	A Huey Helicopter	Courtesy of Randy Parmley. Scan by Minette Siegel.
82	Sculpture by Frederick Hart, near The Vietnam Memorial Wall, Washington, D.C.	Photograph by Carl Gernazio.
84	101st Airborne Pin	Author's Private Collection. Photograph by Minette Siegel.
84	Fellow Army buddies	Author's Private Collection. Photo restoration by Desta Garrett.
88	Two Insignias, Currahee 506th Infantry	Courtesy of Randy Parmley.
93	Two friends, Roy and Gary, playing ball at Phu Bai	Author's Private Collection. Photo restoration by Desta Garrett.
95	Author setting Napalm Charges	Author's Private Collection. Photo restoration by Desta Garrett.
96	Brutus on Bunker Guard Duty	Author's Private Collection. Scan by Minette Siegel.
112	Two letters from Author's Mom	Author's Private Collection. Scan by Minette Siegel.
113	Letter from Author's Godmother, Aunt Leona	Author's Private Collection. Scan by Minette Siegel.
114	View from the Watchtower	Author's Private Collection. Scan by Minette Siegel.
115	Portrait of Bob Dylan	With deepest gratitude to Photographer Baron Wolman.
117	Sunrise view from Watchtower	Author's Private Collection. Scan by Minette Siegel.
119	"Rendezvous With Destiny" Pin	Author's Private Collection. Photograph by Minette Siegel.
120	Sydney, Australia Opera House, 1971	Author's Private Collection. Scan by Minette Siegel.

Page No.	Item	Credit
122	Author swimming	Author's Private Collection. Photo restoration by Desta Garrett.
122	The Texas Tavern Coaster	Author's Private Collection. Scan by Desta Garrett.
123	The Texas Tavern	Author's Private Collection. Scan by Minette Siegel.
123	Australian Money, 1971	Author's Private Collection.
124	Postcard from Author to Family	Author's Private Collection. Scan by Minette Siegel.
125	Author in front of hotel	Author's Private Collection. Scan by Minette Siegel.
136	Roberto Clemente Baseball Card	Author's Private Collection. Permission by Barry Bowen, Licensing, of The Tootsie Roll Co., Chicago, Illinois.
136	"Moon Rat" drawing	Thank you to Ms. Leny Wendel, artist and Samoyed owner, White Bear Lake, MN.
140	Map of North and South Vietnam, circa 1971	Original Art by Brad Johnson.
141	Photograph of Camp Evans	Courtesy of Randy Parmley.
145	Two photos of Army buddies, December 1971	Author's Private Collection. Scans by Minette Siegel.
146	Author and Brutus, December 1971	Author's Private Collection. Scan by Minette Siegel.
146	Short-Timer's Calendar	Courtesy of Randy Parmley.
147–148	Letter and envelope from Author's Dad to his brother, Roman, 1945	Author's Private Collection. Scan by Minette Siegel.
149–150	Three photos, Bob Hope's Christmas Tour	Author's Private Collection. Scan by Minette Siegel.
154	Peasants Tilling a Rice Field	The Image Works, New York. ENOVO756655. Copyrighted picture used with permission and thanks to Lorraine Goonan.
158	*Stars and Stripes*, December 25, 1971	Courtesy of *Stars and Stripes*.© 1971, 2016 *Stars and Stripes*, All Rights Reserved. Thanks to Catharine Giordano.
160–161	"The Kid Is Coming Home" (sanitized version)	Layout and coloration by Desta Garrett.
165	"Old Main," Penn State	Permission of Penn State University, Maureen E. Riddel, Director, Trademark Licensing
180	Surface Mine, Beckley, WVa	Author's Private Collection. Scan by Minette Siegel.
181	Salt Mine, below Lake Erie	Author's Private Collection. Scan by Minette Siegel.
182	Photo of Pittsburgh Pirates Winning the World Series in 1971	The Pittsburgh Pirates Yearbook, 1972. Permission granted by Pittsburgh Pirates Baseball Club, Pittsburgh, Pennsylvania, by Joe Billetdeaux, Director, Promotions and Licensing Department.

Page No.	Item	Credit
183	Penn State Rose Bowl Banner, 1995	Permission of Penn State University, Maureen E. Riddel, Director, Trademark Licensing
184	*"Point of Light Award,"* 1993	Author's Private Collection. Photograph by Minette Siegel.
185	Author and Bride, Samoyed Sled Dog Transportation to Wedding Reception	Author's Private Collection. Scan by Desta Garrett.
187	Brutus and Author, 1971	Author's Private Collection. Scan by Minette Siegel.
187	Portrait of Author and Riley in 2011 at San Francisco Presidio	Photograph by Minette Siegel.
188	Author and wife Celinda in HI	Author's Private Collection. Scan by Minette Siegel.
188	Author and Celinda at "Best In "Show" with Seattle, 2007	Author's Private Collection. Courtesy of photographer, Steven Ross, Chehalis, Washington. Scan by Minette Siegel.
189	Photo of Author and Celinda at a dog show with Riley, Ono, and Mia	Author's Private Collection. Permission granted by Ken O'Brien, photographer, O'Brien Photos, Sacramento, CA. Scan by Minette Siegel.
189	Jim and Celinda at the National Cathedral	Author's Private Collection. Scan by Minette Siegel.
194	B. J. Moses, Medals and Master Blaster Award	Medals Courtesy of Mrs. Sakura Moses and Author's Private Collection from Medals of America Company. Photographs by Minette Siegel.
195	Jim and Celinda in Paris	Author's Private Collection. Scan by Minette Seigel.
196	101st Airborne Cap	Author's Private Collection. Photograph by Minette Siegel.
197	Woodland, Washington View	Author's Private Collection.
199	Two photos of the Oregon Health and Science University, Radiation Oncology	Author's Private Collection.
201	Riley's last show, "On Parade," Judge Tami Lynch and Author	Permission by Randy Roberts, Dog Show Photographer, Leavenworth, WA.
201	Jim Cheskawich, SCA President Pin	Author's Private Collection. Photograph by Minette Siegel.
202	Faithie and Author with Mt. Hood in the background	Courtesy, Dr. Ann Brown, Samoyed owner, Lake Oswego, OR. Scan by Minette Siegel.
202	Rebel with "Cats" program	Author's Private Collection.
202	Honor	Author's Private Collection.
203	Library Books, Mt. Shasta Annex	Photograph by Celinda Cheskawich.
204	Library Room, Mt. Shasta Annex	Photograph by Celinda Cheskawich.
204	Library Books, Woodland, WA Annex	Author's Private Collection.

Page No.	Item	Credit
206	Air Crewman Badge	Author's Private Collection from Medals of America Company.
206	Graveyard Plaque of Ron Dallam, Hebron, Maryland	Photograph by Colleen Dallam.
208	Original ARCOM Medal and Citation with Recent Commemorative Coins	Author's Private Collection with Commemorative Coins on left from Medals of America Company.
209	Crowds at The Vietnam Memorial Wall, Washington, DC	Photograph by Carl Gernazio. Scan by Minette Siegel.
215	Young troops being entertained at Da Nang	Author's Private Collection.
219	Vietnam War Cap and Vietnam Service Medal	Author's Private Collection.
220	In Memoriam, Sculpture by Glenna Goodacre near The Vietnam Memorial Wall, Washington, DC	Photograph by Carl Gernazio. Scan by Minette Siegel.
221, 222, 223	Vietnam War Deaths by Race, Service Branch, Service Component, and Age	"Traveling Vietnam Memorial Wall." Photographs by Celinda Cheskawich.
224	"Gone, but not forgotten"	Photograph by Author, Woodland, Washington Cemetery.
227	Map, "Ho Chi Minh" Trail, 1971	Original Art by Brad Johnson
249	Albany Airport, New York	Photograph by Dave Sage.
253	Riley and Author at *Rex of White Way* book signing	Author's Private Collection. Courtesy of Dan Moir, Store Manager, Hi-School Pharmacy, Woodland, WA.
253	The Maxwell Award, front and back	Author's Private Collection.
254	Author with Cami, Des Moines, Iowa, 2014	Courtesy Joan Luna, SCA breeder, owner, member, AKC Judge. Scan by Minette Siegel.
255 Epilogue	Handout: "Traveling Vietnam Memorial Wall," Siskyou County 2014	Courtesy of Celinda Cheskawich. It shows Poem, "Visit to the Wall" by Michael S. Viehman, and it is with deep and grateful appreciation to Michael S. Viehman for usage of his poem in the book.
Back Cover	Cherry Blossoms Blooming near The Vietnam Memorial Wall	Author's Private Collection.

CREDITS
CHARTS AND STATISTICS

[AUTHOR'S NOTE: All of the below are used by permission unless otherwise noted.]

PAGE NO.	CREDIT
22	Casualties by Age, from "Traveling Vietnam Memorial Wall."
23	"Summary Raw Statistics," from: www.mddkw.3.wix.com/Vietnam-Veterans, Mel Wallace, historian; statistics confirmed by *Vietnam for Dummies* and by U.S. government Veteran Administration Statistics website.
23	Vietnam Veterans dying 10–12 years earlier than national levels, The Internet Site for Veterans' Hour: www.veteranshour.com/vietnamwarstatistics.
170	"GS" (General Schedule Levels) and Military Rank Equivalencies, U.S. Department of Defense, 1974: https://federalsoup/federaldaily.com/forum_posts.asp, Feb. 1, 2011.
221, 222, 223	In Memoriam: Casualties by Race, Service Branch, Service Component, and Age, "Traveling Vietnam Memorial Wall."
228	Appendix 1, *The Vietnam War for Dummies; The World Almanac and Book of Facts 2012;* Wikepedia on Vietnam War, Walter Cronkite, Fall of Saigon, and Jane Fonda.
231	Appendix 2, *Merriam-Webster Collegiate Dictionary*; Wikepedia; *The Vietnam War for Dummies.*
232, 233	Appendix 3, U.S. Army Rank and Insignia, *The World Almanac and Book of Facts,* 2012, World Almanac Books, 132 West 31st Street, NY 10001. Printed and Bound by R R Donnelly, Crawfordsville, IN, 139.
234	Appendix 4, U.S. Army Units, *The World Almanac and Book of Facts.*

CREDITS
INTERNET QUOTES AND CITATIONS

[AUTHOR'S NOTE: All of the below are used by permission unless otherwise noted.]

PAGE NO.	CREDIT
31	Thomas Jefferson, www.brainyquote.com/quotes,keywords/strong.html.
33	Muhammad Ali, www.u-s-history.com, pages /h3723.
37	Gerald Ford pardoning draft dodgers, *Wikipedia:* http://en.wikepedia.org/wiki/Gerald_Ford.
37–38	Eisenhower commentary, from *Dictionary of the Vietnam War,* John Olson, 1988.
38	Kennedy/Johnson escalation, from *The Vietnam War for Dummies*, Ronald B. Frankum and Stephen F. Maxner, 2003.
62	John Milton, "On His Blindness," 1655. Oxford: Clarendon Great Books On Line, New York: Bartleby.com, 1999; www.bartleby.com/101/318.html.
76	George Orwell, quoted about Jean Paul Sartre, "giving him the boot," www.critical-theory.com/george-orwell-trolls-jean-paul-sartre-in-1948.
83	Vietnam soldiers the most educated of all U.S. wars to that point. Capt. Scott Benson, USNR "Ret"; vietnamwarstats;and www.uswings.com/vietnamfacts.asp
87	7 out of 8 soldiers served as support staff; www.nationalvietnamveteransfoundation.org/statistics.html
106	*Princeton Review,* quoted in *USA Today,* August 5, 2013.
107	Drug Use in the Military, *Veterans of Foreign Wars (VFW) Magazine.*
153	Weather statistics: http://weatherspark.com/averages/33993/Hue-Thua-Thien-Hue-Province-Vietnam
191	Prostate cancer diagnosis earlier for Vietnam Veterans than national average. The Internet Site for Veteran's Hour: www.veteranshour.com/vietnamwarstatistics.
206	John Milton, "On His Blindness," 1655. Oxford: Clarendon Great Books On Line, New York: Bartleby.com, 1999; www.bartleby.com/101/318.html.
207	Roberto Clemente, Quote to Ernie Banks, The Major League Baseball TV and Internet Video Network, Series on Latin American Players, Hosted by Bob Costas, circa 2013, "Interview with Ernie Banks recalling words from Roberto Clemento to him," early 1960s.
225	*Waging Peace and War: Dean Rusk in the Truman, Kennedy, Johnson Years* by Thomas J. Schoenbaum, per *The New York Times* Book Review 1988.
225	Woods, Randall, *LBJ: Architect of America Ambition,* New York: Free Press, 2006; quoted at Lyndon B. Johnson, *Wikepedia,* The Free Encyclopedia, en.wikepedia.org/wiki/Lyndon_B_Johnson. Quote for "Hey, Hey, LBJ! How Many…?" [December 19, 2013]

Page No.	Credit
226	Robert McNamara, former Secretary of Defense, *The Fog of War,* recipient, 2004 Academy Award for "Best Documentary," Errol Morris, Producer/Director, and *The Unknown Known,* documentary about Donald Rumsfeld, former Secretary of Defense, also Errol Morris, Producer/Director. Plus: Book, *In Retrospect* by Robert McNamara.
226	Dwight D. Eisenhower on "War," published in *Eisenhower Speaks: Dwight D. Eisenhower in His Messages and Speeches*, edited by Rudolph Truenfels, NY: Tarrar, Straus, 1948. wikiquote.org/wiki/Dwight_D_Eisenhower_Speech_in_Ottawa,_January_10_1946.
229	Appendix 1: Lyndon Johnson re: Walter Cronkite, Wikipedia on Walter Cronkite, 1968; http://en.wikipedia.org/wiki/WalterCronkite.
255	With gratitude and immense appreciation to Michael S. Viehman, Excerpt from his poem "Visit to the Wall," from "Traveling Vietnam Memorial Wall."

Lyrics

Page No.	Item
6 Dedication	With deepest appreciation to *Judy Collins,* her team of Erin Bockman and Katherine DePaul at rockymountainproductionsinc.com and Troy Schreck on behalf of Alfred Publishing Company for permission to use the lyrics of *Sons of* by Gerard Jouannest, Jacques Roman Brel, Eric Blau, and Mort Shuman ©1968 (Renewed), Editions Pouchenel S.P.R.L. and Unichappell Music, Inc.
115	To *Bob Dylan,* the greatest songwriter and singer who spoke for our generation, and his team of Jeff Rosen and Callie Gladman, for permission to use the lyrics to *All Along the Watchtower,* written by Bob Dylan, ©1968 by Dwarf Music, renewed 1996 by Dwarf Music.

REFERENCES AND SOURCES
[Page Numbers in brackets are to this present manuscript.]

Brooks, Rodney, "Can You Really Find a Job in Retirement?" *USA Today,* August 27, 2013, Gannett, Larry Kramer-President and Publisher, McLean, VA.

Cheskawich, Jim, *The Story of Rex of White Way:The Blizzard King,* Woodland, WA, Rex the Blizzard King Stories, LLC, November 2012. [95, 96, 200, 250]

Francis, Mike, "Oregon Veterans Fight VA for Compensation," *The Oregonian,* July 5, 2013 [152, 179]

Frankum, Ronald B., Jr. and Stephen F. Maxner, *The Vietnam War for Dummies,* Wiley Publishing Inc., NY, 2003. [22, 23, 37, 38, 87, 90, 116, 144, 153, 205, 206, 228, 229, 230, 231]

Gibson, Kelly, "Veteran Stereotypes Misguided," *Veterans of Foreign War Magazine,* August 2013, Published by Veterans of Foreign Wars of the United States, Kansas City, MO. [106, 107]

Hampson, Rick, *USA Today,* July 3–4, 2013, Gannett, "Vets Wonder if N. Korea Threats Will Force Us To "Do It All Over Again," Larry Kramer, President and Publisher, McLean, VA.

Hayslip, Le Ly, with Jay Hurts, *When Heaven and Earth Changed Places,* The Penguin Group, NY, May 1990.

Janssen, Sarah, *The World Almanac and Book of Facts*, World Almanac Books, NY, 2012. [221, 222, 223, 225, 227, 228, 229, 230, 232, 233, 234]

McNamara, Robert S., *In Retrospect: The Tragedy and Lessons of Vietnam*, Vintage Books, NY, 1995. [20, 36, 37, 226]

McPherson, James, *Battle Cry of Freedom: The Civil War Era,* Oxford University Press, NY, 1988. [156]

Merriam-Webster's *Collegiate Dictionary* 11th Edition, Frederick C. Mish, Editor-in-Chief. Springfield, MA: Merriam-Webster, Incorporated, 2004. [230, 231, 232, 233]

Merton, Thomas, *The Seven Storey Mountain,* Harcourt Brace & Company, NY, 1948. [76]

Murray, Aaron R., *Vietnam War Battles and Leaders*, DK Publishing Inc., NY, 2004. [37, 38, 59, 144, 227, 228, 229, 230]

Murray, Stuart, *Vietnam War,* Eyewitness Books, DK Publishing, NY, May 16, 2005. [37, 38, 144, 206]

Olson, James S., *Dictionary of the Vietnam War,* Greenwood Press, Westport, CN, 1988. [37, 38, 59, 153, 205, 206, 227]

101 History of the Screaming Eagles, A Publication of the 101st Airborne Division (Airmobile), circa 1969. [32, 58, 59, 65]

Obituary for Curtis Tarr, age 88, who oversaw the draft lottery for the Selective Service System during the Vietnam War. He instituted the system based on birthdays that were picked on national TV. *The Sunday Oregonian,* June 30, 2013, Portland, OR. [34, 37]

Pacific Stars and Stripes, An Authorized Unofficial Publication for the Armed Forces of the Pacific Command, Various Dates between January 1971–January 1972. [79, 158]

Princeton Review, "Ranking of U.S. Colleges and Universities as Party Schools," *USA Today,* August 5, 2013, Larry Kramer-President and Publisher, McLean, VA. [106]

Reich, Charles A., *The Greening of America,* New York, Randon House, Inc., 1970. [105]

Steinman, Ron, *The Soldiers' Story: Vietnam in Their Own Words,* Self-published, Circa 1980.

Taylor, David W., *American Legion Magazine,* "How Did We Get Such Good Men?" June 2013. Published by The American Legion, Indianapolis, IN. [22, 23, 24, 25, 83, 84, 85, 102, 107, 143, 207]

United States Army Infantry Training Center Brochure, Fort Ord, California. Published for the U.S. Army, circa 1968. [47]

Vonnegut, Kurt, *Slaughter House Five,* NY: Delacort, 1969. [Author's inspiration for 21]

Zoroya, Gregg, *USA Today,* "Warriors Without a War," November 4, 2013, Larry Kramer-President and Publisher, Gannett, McLean, VA. [156, 163]

Zoroya, Gregg, *USA Today,* "War Vets Can't Get Their Hands On Benefits," June 12, 2013, Larry Kramer-President and Publisher, Gannett, McLean, VA. [153]

INTERNET SOURCES
[NOTE: Dates at the end in brackets are when the Web links were accessed.
Page Numbers in brackets are to this present manuscript.]

Ali, Muhammad, Quote on Refusing to Fight: www.u-s-history.com/pages/h3723.html. [January 5, 2014, 33]

Average Weather for Hue, Vietnam: WeatherSpark: http://weatherspark.com/averages/33993/Hue-Thua-Thien-Hue-Province-Vietnam. [August 28, 2013, 99]

B-2/501ST Inf (101st Abn Div) RVN 67–72, at: www.b2501airborne.com. [November 29, 2013]

Beaton, Capt. Scott, USNR (Ret.) and Statistical Source, "Vietnam War: Facts, Stats & Myths," reference to "most highly educated": www.uswings.com/vietnamfacts.asp. [December 23, 2013, 22, 23, 83, 191]

Clemente, Roberto, Quote to Ernie Banks, The Major League Baseball TV and Internet Video Network, Series on Latin American Players, Hosted by Bob Costas, circa 2013, "Interview with Ernie Banks recalling words from Roberto Clemento to him," early 1960s. [207]

Collins, Judy, "Sons Of" song," from Whales and Nightingales Album 1970, http://www.maxilyrics.com/judy-collins-sons-of-lyrics-0e47.html. [September 21, 2013, 6]

Cronkite, Walter, Vietnam Visit and Pres. Johnson's remarks about Cronkite's television editorial (Timeline): Wikipedia on Walter Cronkite, 1968: http://en.wikipedia.org/wiki/Walter_Cronkite. [February 25, 2014, 229]

Dylan, Bob, Lyrics—"All Along the Watchtower," Dwarf Music ©1968, renewed 1996: www.azlyrics.com/lyrics/bobdylan/allalongthewatchtower.html. [December 12, 2013, 115]

Eisenhower, Dwight D. Published in *Eisenhower Speaks: Dwight D. Eisenhower in His Messages and Speeches,* Edited by Rudolph Treuenfels, NY: Farrar, Straus, 1948. wikiquote.org/wiki/Dwight_D_Eisenhower_Speech_in_Ottawa,_January_10,_1946. [226]

Federal Soup/Federal Daily: Geneva Convention Military and Civilian Equivalent Grades, October 15, 2013: https://federalsoup.federaldaily.com/forum_posts.aspFeb1,2011. [170]

Ford, Gerald, *Wikepedia,* The Free Encyclopedia, en.wikepedia.org/wiki/Gerald_Ford, Pardon of Draft Dodgers on September 16, 1974, Presidential Proclamation 4313, p.12/38 on website. [January 5, 2014, 34, 37]

Hanson, Capt. Marshal, U.SN.R. (Ret.), *The Beat Post,* "Interesting Thoughts and Facts About Viet Nam Vets," September 11, 2013: www.bentbay.dk/abe_wooda_thought.html. [83, 85, 102]

Ho Chi Minh, wikipedia-Hochiminh,en.wikipedia.org/wiki.org/hochiminh,_February_14,_2005. [February 5, 2015, 227]

Ho Chi Minh Trail, http://en.wikepedia.org/wiki.org/Hochiminhtrail [February 5, 2015, 227].

Jefferson, Thomas, quote on "Strong body and strong Mind": www.brainyquote.com/quotes/keywords/strong.html. [January 5, 2014, 31.]

Lee, Robert E. "Son of the South," Quotes, Lee quote about war: www.sonofthesouth.net/leefoundation/NotableLeeQuotes.htm. [December 23, 2013. [25]

Loy, Jim, Phu Bai Topical Heading: www.jimloy.com/jim/phubai.htm. [September 8, 2013, 59, 69, 86, 87, 88, 89, 90, 91, 99]

Milton, John, 1608–1674, "On His Blindness," Oxford: Clarendon Great Books on Line (Free of Charge), New York: Bartleby.com, 1999, www.bartleby.com/101/318.html. [August 24, 2013, 62, 206]

Moonrat, information on habitat, description, *Wikipedia*: http://en.wikepedia.org/wiki/moonrat. [February 5, 2015, 136]

Navy Department Library, The, Military Rank Equivalency and Comparison of Military and Civilian Equivalent Grades, www.history.navy.mil/library/online/comparison. [October 15, 2013, 170]

New York Times Book Review: Schoenbaum, Thomas J. *Waging Peace and War: Dean Rusk in the Truman, Kennedy, and Johnson Years.* New York: Simon and Schuster, 1988. htttp://www.nytimes.com/1988/07/17books/a-good-man-in-a-bad-war-html. [225]

101st Airborne Division Arrives in Vietnam, "This Day in History"—7/29/1965: www.history.com/this-day-in-history/101st-airborne-division-arrives-in-vietnam. [July 29, 2013, 38, 58, 59, 144]

101st Airborne Division, "chicken men" and "over 20,000 wounded or killed." *Wikipedia*, the Free Encyclopedia, at http://en.wikipedia.org/wiki/101st_Airborne_Division. [July 1, 2013, 59, 99, 144]

Orwell, George, Quote about Jean Paul Sartre, "giving him the boot," www.critical-theory.com/george-orwell-trolls-jean-paul-sartre-in-1948. [76]

Phoenix Army Aviation, at: http://uccr.tripod.com/vietnam/phoenix.html. [July 1, 2013]

Reagan, President Ronald, "Interview with President Ronald Reagan," Internet video: "A Soldier's Pledge," now.msn.com/freedom-isn't-free. "This moving video with Ronald Reagan tells us why." [July 14, 2013, Author's inspiration for 9]

Robbins, Tony, quote on conditions, decisions, and destiny: www.goodreads.com/author/show/5627anthony_robbins. [December 15, 2013, 20]

Viet Cong: http://en.wikipedia.org/wiki/viet_cong. [231]

Vietnam War Statistics: www.nationalvietnamveteransfoundation.org/statistics/html. [22, 83, 87]

Wikepedia on "Terms, Phrases, Products": http://en.wikipedia.org/wiki/Tang_(drink). [February 27, 2014, 231]

U.S. Naval Mobile Construction Battalion 121 History: http://mcb121.com/history.htm. [July 1, 2013, 230]

Vietnam War Statistics, U.S. Government (VA Web Site Stats): www.veteranshour.com/vietnam_war_statistics.htm. [December 23, 2013, 22, 23, 25, 83, 191]

Vonnegut, Kurt, quote on writing what you know and quickly: www.imdb.com/name/nm0903361/bio. [December 17, 2013, 18]

Wallace, Mel, "Vietnam Veterans Dying at an Earlier Age": mddkw3.wix.com/Vietnam-Veterans. [December 23, 2013, 19, 21, 23, 102, 153, 190, 191]

Welcome to the 8th Radio Research Field Station, Phu Bai, Viet Nam at: www.cswayne.com/nam.html. [July 1, 2013, 99]

Woods, Randall, *LBJ: Architect of America Ambition,* New York: Free Press, 2006; quoted at Lyndon B. Johnson, *Wikepedia,* The Free Encyclopedia, en.wikipedia.org/wiki/Lyndon_B_Johnson. Quote for "Hey, Hey, LBJ! How Many…?" [December 19, 2013, 227]

Woodstock Music Festival, *Wikepedia*, (Timeline): http://en.wikipedia.org/wiki/Woodstock_Music_Festival, on Woodstock Music Festival. [February 25, 2014, 231]

ACKNOWLEDGMENTS
AND
CHRONOLOGY OF BOOK

**Albany Airport, New York, where I drafted the first seven pages of my book!
Photograph by Dave Sage.**

I am indebted to Shawn Link and Kathy Bounds of La Center High School for lending me their Vietnam class materials and allowing me to substitute-teach in their classrooms for nearly thirteen years. I am also grateful to all of their students for their probing questions. I told the classes many times that Mrs. Bounds "knew more about the War than I did."

The truth is that I did not want to know more for nearly four decades—as I had my fill of Vietnam, and I will admit that after starting the background work, that first week the bad dreams began to reappear, although they subsided as I moved through it and began to write more and more.

My Editor, Vicki Weiland (also Editor of my first book, *The Story of Rex of White Way,*

The Blizzard King, released in 2012), was a constant source of support. She encouraged me

in 2013 when I started writing the book to always try to keep writing. I did quit on the book

for two weeks. Then I picked up my notes again, and while reviewing and "packing-up" the

reference materials, once again I was certain that I did *not* want to write for anyone about what I

did and how I *feel!* Only now, I was afraid of being "too honest."

This was something that several Veterans (who are current members in The Samoyed Club

of America) assured me could not possibly occur!

"How valuable would your memoir be," they asked me, *"if you hold back?"*

Then I knew that I would almost be writing fiction—through deliberate understatement.

I reflected on this and reasoned that if I painted a fuller picture, maybe other Veterans

could see themselves in my story and maybe readers from any walk of life could learn from

my mistakes. Those of us who served in Vietnam or any war have to find meaning and purpose

to survive day to day. You can't live spontaneously looking for excitement and taking high risk

behavior in a war zone—if you want to survive or enhance your chance of surviving.

I soon looked forward to writing this book each day. Once I started writing, I never

really developed "writer's block" and never had to throw away any uncompleted work! My

Editor used to say to give her *more rather than less,* as, otherwise, she would never know what

I left out. I wanted to enjoy the writing process so I limited myself to one to two hours a day of

writing, which allowed for writing, ongoing research, reflection, rewriting, and editing. To begin

each new day of writing, I would first review what I had typed in the previous session. Years

ago, I realized I like the editing and reediting process almost as much as writing the first draft. I

hadn't planned to finish the first draft in seven weeks but that's how it developed. I could have

written for three to four hours a day but I wanted to limit myself so I would not appear to write

carelessly or endlessly.

To help me stay focused, my two Samoyeds—Riley and Honor—were usually within

arm's reach on the floor next to the small card-table-sized kitchen table where I did almost all of my work. Research books and maps were always close at hand on an adjacent table.

Interruptions for phone calls infrequently occurred and didn't really distract me from my reverie.

I guess I had a lot of practice in my government jobs with phone calls and meetings.

I had a pastoral view during most of the day, living on the aptly named "Butte Hill," and

I frequently paused to look at the alpacas and cats next door, or the occasional hawk or owl

that was out for a meal. The elk herd, deer, and coyotes don't usually appear until winter in my

orchard and they stuck to their schedule while I wrote this book. But I looked for them anyway.

I have windows on three sides of the kitchen which afford me ample viewing of the many

Douglas firs that reach well over 200-feet into the sky and surround half the house. The morning

fog in the Lewis River Valley below the house served to obscure the rolling hills of farmland and

evergreens usually visible off in the distance. The top 800-feet of Mt. Hood in Oregon appears

from the south side of my house, whenever the mountain wants to "come out." Evening sunsets

which reflect orange-pink off of snow-capped Mt. Hood help contribute to a peaceful setting

which facilitates reflective writing.

With the help of Oregon's all-classical radio station (89.9 FM)—which I listened to 95%

of the time while I researched and typed—my first draft was finished in seven weeks.

Sometimes I stopped work to listen to the *William Tell Overture* or the *1812 Overture*. I

think Riley could tell when the "Theme for the Lone Ranger" was playing, as he seemed to start

looking around for "Silver." Honor liked to lay squarely on her back whenever Bach was playing.

I can see how the music affects the dogs; it also had an effect on me. Even though I was

writing about the Rolling Stones, CCR, Big Brother and the Holding Company, Jethro Tull, and

Jimi Hendrix, my thoughts needed to develop freely without artificially-induced jagged edges or

angst created by the music. **Vietnam is a serious topic—even under the best of circumstances—**

and I needed a conducive and supportive atmosphere to record and filter my thoughts.

After delaying the start of the book long enough, I pulled out the laptop from my attaché

case on August 2, 2013 as I had an eight-hour wait at the Albany, NY Airport for a connecting

flight back to Portland, Oregon. I had my first seven pages drafted within a few hours! With a few days taken to sub-teach in the new school year, I finished my first draft in Woodland, Washington on September 24, 2013.

I thank all of those involved in helping me finish and edit the book: the Vets who shared their stories with me and who helped me to "open up" more in the book as I noticed common themes that appeared in each of our stories. Also, to Dave Sage, David and Marion Gustafson, Annie Reid, Joan Luna, Kathy Mackai, Mary Kistner, Susan Amundson, Suzanne Marie Stuart, and others who offered substantive or encouraging comments or feedback.

I want to express special thanks to Celinda Cheskawich for her many photographs and ongoing support. I want to thank Carl Gernazio for photographs of The Vietnam Memorial Wall and Statues in Washington, DC; I would also like to thank Ken O'Brien, O'Brien's Photos, Sacramento, CA; Steven Ross Photography, Chehalis, Washington; Dr. Ann Brown, Samoyed owner, Lake Oswego, Oregon; and Randy Roberts, Dog Show Photographer, Leavenworth, Washington.

I thank Pat Palmer and staff of Speedy Litho/Copies Today of Kelso, Washington for their superlative work on the mockups. Thank you also to Catharine Gordano of *Stars and Stripes* for permission to use two images. Also my thanks to Elise Gochberg and Marlous Fehr of Friesens.

Also my sincere thanks to the late *Muhammad Ali,* and his staff, for the photo of Muhammad Ali - Sonny Liston.

I would also like to deeply thank world reknown photographer, *Baron Wolman,* for his iconic pictures of Janis Joplin, Jimi Hendrix, and Bob Dylan.

Also I give thanks to *Michael S. Viehman* for his Poem, "Visit to the Wall," on "Traveling Vietnam Memorial Wall," and to John Devitt, Norris Shears, Gerry Hauer, and other Vietnam Veteran volunteers (builders) of "Traveling Vietnam Memorial Wall."

I also express my heartfelt appreciation to *Judy Collins*, her team of Erin Bockman and Katherine DePaul at rockymountainproductionsinc.com and to Troy Schreck on behalf of Alfred Publishing Company for permission to use the lyrics of *Sons of* by Brel, Jouannest, Blau, Shuman, Editions Pouchenel S.P.R.L. and Unichappell, Music, Inc.

And to the greatest songwriter and singer who spoke for our generation, *Bob Dylan*, and his team of Jeff Rosen and Callie Gladman for permission to use the lyrics to *All Along the Watchtower.*

I would like to extend a special thank-you to Kristie Kempker of Visually Speaking for her excellent professional services in transferring the entire book into Kindle and CreateSpace formats.

My thanks also to my Team: Desta Garrett (book production and layout); Minette Siegel (Image Director); Vicki Weiland (book development and design); Brad Johnson (designer, Vietnam maps). Special thanks to Randy Parmley for the Front Cover Photo of "Huey's On a Combat Air Assault" and to Tamara Somerville for the Front Cover Photo of The Vietnam Memorial Wall; and to all others who brought their individual expertise together to help me to create my Vietnam "memoir and reflections" book.

On a special note, as I learned from the success of *The Story of Rex of White Way, The Blizzard King,* when you have a great Team, you stick with it! I knew where I needed help and knew what each Team member would bring. Without *Rex*, there would be no Vietnam memoir book. And, although I purposely tried to keep my voice hidden in *Rex*, it is *here* … in this subsequent book.

Riley and Jim at a *Rex of White Way* book signing.

The Maxwell Award, 2013, to Jim Cheskawich.

ABOUT THE AUTHOR

At 68 years old, Jim Cheskawich is an author, speaker, an American Kennel Club "Breeder of Merit," and "Trademarked" dog-kennel owner. He served in South Vietnam with the 101st Airborne Division and later worked twenty-eight years in a variety of personnel positions with the Federal Government in Washington, DC. He retired in 2002 as the Human Resources Director for Mine Safety and Health Administration with the U.S. Department of Labor.

His non-profit work experience includes: serving as President and Treasurer for The Samoyed Club of America (SCA) and he has been a part of its "Education and Research Foundation" for almost fifteen years. Jim owns and manages Woodland Kennels in Woodland, WA and sub-teaches in K–12 grades in four school districts in southwest Washington

Jim Cheskawich and Cami (a Rex descendant), and winner of "Award of Merit" at The Samoyed Club of America National Specialty, September 2014, Des Moines, Iowa.

State. He is an Assistant Football Coach at La Center High School, seasons 2015 and 2016.

He has a B.S. in Business Management and an MBA from Pennsylvania State University and is an Alumni member. He is also a member of the Camas, WA Post of the Veterans of Foreign Wars.

His first book, *The Story of Rex of White Way: The Blizzard King* won Gold and Silver e-book medals in addition to the 2013 "The Maxwell Award" from the Dog Writers' Association of America. He has sold 3,000++ books (hardback and softback and Kindle) since its publication in 2012. In 2014, he founded and was the first President of "The Rex of White Way Samoyed Memorial Library and Museum." Nationwide donations of Samoyed books, magazines, and pictures have given the Library a strong beginning.

This book on Vietnam is the culmination of *making peace* with his experiences, and his next steps include promoting it, meeting and sharing with others, and living his life with memories of Vietnam *alongside*, but not impeding, it … anymore.

EPILOGUE

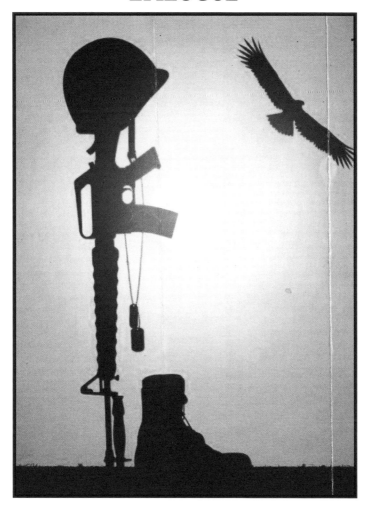

Brothers…
You will go to THE Wall soon.…
We will be together sooner
    than we can imagine.
The Spirits at the Wall know this…
I figure they all look forward to it…
But all in good time…

If we've been left behind,
It's because we still have a mission.
May the spirit of the brothers at
The Wall
Help you find your mission-your
Reason for being.

You/we lived-for luck or for reason –
I think our brothers know the reason.

I swear to you my Brothers…
When you touch that Wall…
Your long lost Brothers…
Will reach into your soul with healing…

Accept it – for you & for them…
It is all they want of you.
It is all they want for you…

– Michael S. Viehman

Excerpt from Poem, "Visit to the Wall,"from Traveling Vietnam Memorial Wall.
From Handout, Siskiyou County 2014.

UNIQUE

VIETNAM 1971: REMEMBERING THE "101ˢᵗ" *THEN* AND *NOW*

This book follows the life journey of an "All American Boy" before, during, and post-Vietnam War. Born in Pennsylvania into a lower-class family, Author Jim Cheskawich attended Penn State on Social Security benefits, was drafted by the "Lottery" (Number "82") to serve in Vietnam, and returned home with "PTSD" (but who *knew it*, since it didn't have a name then). He married (which ended in an amicable divorce), had a 28-year career with the federal government, and is now involved in the 'Dog Show World' of Samoyeds. He has suffered two bouts of cancer caused by exposure to *Agent Orange,* with surgery and radiation provided through the Veterans Administration.

This book traces it all and also, how now, Jim is *"at peace" at last,* with his time in Vietnam and its long-term impacts.

Yet, as Jim states in the book, "Most Vietnam Veterans do *not* like to talk about the War, even today, and it has taken me *forty-four years* to begin to do so!"

He then relates the following: "Since I substitute-teach high school in my home area of Woodland, Washington and often times American History is among the topics, *I am always asked about Vietnam by my students,* because their fathers and grandfathers have been silent. What I know is that when we who served are all gone, there will be no one to say what the Vietnam War zone was like. *Vietnam* is one of the most negative words in our country. The time is *now* to break out of this pattern and to move into 'open dialogue.' I believe that this will *help* Vietnam Veterans, their families, and friends to *heal*."

Vietnam 1971: Remembering The "101ˢᵗ" Then And Now allows readers of all ages to experience what the 1960s and 1970s were like. There are over eighty photos of the time and seasons, including famous iconic photos of Janis Joplin, Jimi Hendrix, and Bob Dylan by *Baron Wolman,* and *on site Vietnam photos* by the Author, including the visit of the "Bob Hope Performers."

In hearing about this book as it was being written, fellow Vietnam Veterans urged, *"You have to tell the truth!"*

In providing his personal story, from *his* personal perspective, Author Jim Cheskawich has done just that.